ordinary people

do you find, as I do, that somehow despite its familiarity the Christmas story never loses its appeal? In a world dominated by brand names, celebrities and the centrality of 'image', it reminds us that God's values are completely different. God chose to communicate the good news of great joy to a small group of poor shepherds, calling them to visit a family where a birth had just taken place. Hardly the sort of event that would interest the media! Yet it is ordinary people like these who are the focus of God's attention. This issue's articles consider three themes related to these events: great news shared in small groups, God's concern for the poor and the key role of families.

The Rt Rev David Urquhart argues forthrightly that 'a church that meets people's real needs cannot fail to appeal.' One way we can do this is by emphasising the importance of small groups for disciple-making and evangelisation. Scripture Union is concerned to encourage such groups, providing resourcing and support – you might like to have a look at church@home on the SU website – www.scriptureunion.org.uk – a mine of information.

Ross Pilkinton, one of our regular writers, tells us movingly of some turning points in his life, especially how God turned his heart towards the poor of Metro Manila and Nepal. Also, Keith Civval, Chief Executive of SU England and Wales, brings before us the needs of families in our societies today and renews SU's commitment to the strengthening of family life.

This quarter we welcome Fergus Macdonald to the writing team. He brings a wealth of experience, reflected in his helpful comments.

Andrew C. Clark

PS: Please note the changes in price detailed in full on p128. From January 2004, individual issues will be £2.99 each, or £11 for a year in the UK. When thinking about Christmas presents, you might like to consider *Encounter with God: Every Day for a Year*. A handsome hardback with a selection of the best of the last four years' notes, it's a bargain at only £9.99 for 416 pages (ISBN 1 85999 670 1).

the writers

○ **Whitney Kuniholm** is President of Scripture Union in the USA, and has written a number of books on personal and group Bible study. He is married to Carol and has three children.

○ **Rev Ross Pilkinton** lives in New Zealand. He worked until recently as a missionary in Pokhara, Nepal.

○ **Rev Dr John Harris** is Director of the Translation and Text Division of the Bible Society in Australia. His major interest is in Australian and Pacific languages and the faithful transmission of the Scriptures in those cultures.

○ **Rev Fergus Macdonald** is a minister in the Free Church of Scotland, and recently retired as General Secretary of the United Bible Societies. He is particularly interested in encouraging engagement with the Bible among those who find it and the Christian church to be irrelevant.

○ **Rt Rev Michael Baughen** acts as Assistant Bishop in the Anglican Diocese of London. He was Bishop of Chester from 1982 to 1996.

○ **Rt Rev David Urquhart** is Anglican Bishop of Birkenhead and Chairman of the Trustees for the Church Mission Society.

○ **David Blair** has worked in Scripture Union England and Wales' schools and Bible ministries departments, and also worked to pioneer SU's work in Central and Eastern Europe. He is married to Valerie.

○ **Dr Pauline Hoggarth** is Bible Ministries Co-ordinator for Scripture Union International. Her interests include cooking, gardening, cinema and conversation. She attends an Episcopal church in Scotland.

○ **Rev Dr Steve Motyer** is Lecturer in New Testament and Hermeneutics at London Bible College. He enjoys cycling and gardening, and supports his wife, a highly stressed social worker, as much as possible.

○ **Keith Civval** is Chief Executive and Team Leader for Scripture Union England and Wales, having previously pursued a career in financial services in the City of London. He lives in Hertfordshire and attends an Anglican church.

○ **John Grayston** is Director of Bible Ministries for Scripture Union in England and Wales, and is involved in leadership at a Baptist church.

○ **Rev Vera Sinton** teaches theology part-time at the Oxford Centre for Youth Ministry. She works in parish ministry and as a Christian counsellor.

using these notes

e *ncounter with God* provides you with a systematic, thought-provoking approach to Bible reading, enabling you to explore Scripture's relevance to us and our society with the help of an international team of scholars and writers:

- *Systematic.* You will read through the New Testament every four years, and the Old Testament every six. This provides the opportunity to develop a broad understanding of how Scripture fits together, and of its underlying story.
- *Thought-provoking.* We aim not to retell the contents of a biblical passage, but to pose and answer the questions that come naturally to readers' minds. We believe that in the long run you will build up a variety of Bible reading skills, and be able to use them with confidence.
- *Relevant.* We hope you will be encouraged to see the Bible's teaching as having an important impact, not just on our personal spiritual lives, but also on issues of global concern.

Each set of readings begins with an *Introduction*, which should enable you to set each reading in its biblical context. The *Taking it further* pages are designed to help you think through and respond to the themes highlighted by the writers, while the *Prepare* and *Respond* sections at the start and end of each note offer opportunities for you to pause for reflection and prayer.

Encounter with God is based on the NIV translation of the Bible, but can easily be used with any other Bible version.

Scripture quotations from the NIV © 1973, 1978, 1984 by International Bible Society. Anglicisation copyright © 1979, 1984, 1989. Used by permission of Hodder and Stoughton Limited.

Scripture quotations from *The Message* © by Eugene H Peterson 1993, 1994, 1995, 1996. Used by permission of NavPress Publishing Group.

© Scripture Union 2003. 207–209 Queensway, Bletchley, Milton Keynes MK2 2EB. Website: www.scriptureunion.org.uk Design by MHM Grax. Images supplied by Photodisc. Printed by Ebenezer Baylis & Son Ltd. ISSN 1350-5130

Scripture Union is an international Christian charity working with churches in more than 130 countries providing resources to bring the good news about Jesus Christ to children, young people and families – and to encourage them to develop spiritually through the Bible and prayer. As well as our network of volunteers, staff and associates who run holidays, church-based events and school Christian groups, we produce a wide range of publications and support those who use our resources through training programmes.

meeting God

come to God

Come to the Lord as you are. Worship him for his power, greatness and majesty. Bring him your feelings and needs. Ask for his Holy Spirit to help you to understand and respond to what you read.

read

Read the Bible passage slowly and thoughtfully, listening out for what God is saying to you.

talk with God

Talk to God about what you have read. These suggestions may help you:

- 'Lord, thank you for your Word to me today. What special message are you shouting out to me, or whispering to me, in these verses?'

- 'Lord, I want to meet you here; tell me more about yourself, Father, Son and Holy Spirit, in these verses.'

- 'I don't know what today holds for me, Lord. I need your guidance, your advice. I need you to help me be alert. Direct my heart and thoughts to those words you know I need.'

- 'Lord, your Word is a mirror in which I often find myself. Show me myself here, as you see me, alone or with others. Thank you that you understand how I feel as I read your Word.'

- 'Lord, there are things here I don't understand. Please help me through the SU guide, or give me others who may help me.'

respond

Try to find a key thought or phrase which has come to you from this passage to carry with you through the day. Pray for people who are on your mind at the moment. Determine to share your experiences with others.

contents

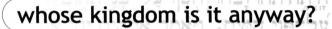

whose kingdom is it anyway?

Oriiginally combined as one book, 1 and 2 Kings take us on a journey that begins at the high point in Israel's history – the reign of its two greatest kings, David and Solomon – and ends at the lowest point for the chosen people – the fall of Jerusalem and the destruction of the Temple. In between those two points is a substantial period of about 400 years. We are introduced to a succession of Israel's leaders, from both the northern and southern kingdoms. In the process, we have the opportunity to contemplate the decisions made by each, under all kinds of pressure – family jealousy, military attacks, political manoeuvring, and the ever-present temptation to worship idols. In the midst of all this royal drama, 1 and 2 Kings zero in on the key factor that ultimately determined the fate of each leader; it's the same factor that determines our effectiveness in the Christian life today. Those who were successful 'did what was right in the eyes of the Lord' and those who failed 'did what was evil in the eyes of the Lord.' It sounds so simple but the challenge both then and now is to choose God's way, no matter what.

Our first six readings examine a critical time for Israel's monarchy – the handing of power from David to Solomon. There is much to be admired about how this happened – in particular, David's emphasis on obeying God (2:2–3) and Solomon's famous request for wisdom (3:7–10). But there are warnings for us as well, in particular about the long-term consequences of even just a little sin (3:3). Our readings also raise some interesting questions. For example, how important is human wisdom? Solomon asked for it and God was pleased with his request. But is that what makes a great leader? By the end of his reign, Solomon seems to have been tempted by the trappings of his own success (11:1–13). Perhaps the lesson is that human wisdom is important and valuable, but the more important thing is to have a heart that is totally committed to following God. Another question raised here is why are we so willing to compromise with sin, even though we know the consequences? Surely Solomon was smart enough to know that a little idol worship would only lead to more. But he did it anyway (3:3 – see note in 'further reading', below). Even today, many followers of Christ are afraid to be seen as different; some want to prove that Christians can 'be like everyone else.' Really? The reality is that when we've committed our lives to Christ, we belong to a different kingdom. The best way to prevent sin from getting hold of us is to stop trying to be like everybody else and to focus instead on trying to be like Jesus.

A final question worth pondering is why was it so difficult for Israel's leaders to 'finish well?' For that matter, is it really possible for any Christian to remain completely faithful to God for the long haul? The answer is, 'No, not in our own strength.' The truth is, all of us have sinned; all of us have and will fall short of the glory of God.[1] David learned this the hard way.[2] But fortunately, he also learned the secret to finishing well – the willingness to repent and start over with renewed commitment to following God's ways.[3] It's easy to criticise our leaders when they make mistakes. 'I can't believe what they've done now.' But it's much harder to face the temptations of being in charge and have the responsibility to make the right choices under pressure. It's a reminder worth considering the next time we are tempted to criticise our church leaders. It would be much better if our first instinct was not to criticise, but to pray for them.

Whitney Kuniholm

further reading
Iain W Provan, *1 and 2 Kings*, NIBC, Paternoster, 1995; Donald J Wiseman, *1 and 2 Kings*, TOTC, Leicester, IVP, 1993 – for a fuller discussion of the relationship between the 'high places' and idol worship, see pp82–83 of this book.

1 Rom 3:23 **2 2 Sam 11:1–27** **3 2 Sam 12:13; Ps 51**

mind your own business?

What do you want to achieve in life? What do you want to be recognised for? Why?

1 Kings 1:1-27

adonijah would have no trouble getting elected to political office today. He was bold and ambitious (v 5), secured key endorsements (v 7), and understood the value of public relations (vs 5,9). But that's not the path to spiritual leadership, as he would soon find out. What fuelled Adonijah's lust for power? Certainly pride had something to do with it ('*I* will be king…', v 5). And he probably felt a sense of jealous indignation; as David's oldest living son he no doubt sensed his father's preference for his younger half-brother Solomon. But our text inserts an interesting clue: David never challenged Adonijah's apparently questionable behaviour; he 'never interfered with him' (v 6). For all his natural ability, Adonijah may simply have been desperate for his father's love and attention. Many parents take a hands-off view about providing guidance to their teenaged children: 'Well, I guess there's nothing I can really do any more.' But that's a huge mistake. Young people, whoever they are, need adults who care enough to question their behaviour in love. And when we hold others accountable for their actions it puts the spotlight on our own behaviour as well.

Nathan wasn't interested in power, but notice the influential way he communicated with David (vs 11–14, 24–27). It was respectful, creative and he allowed David to come to his own conclusion, a skill he had used before.[1] We can't force young people or adults to make the right choices, but we can show them that we care enough to notice when they head in the wrong direction, and we can love them enough to say something respectfully and creatively when they do. That's what Christian community is all about.

Many successful adults are still desperate for attention and love from their fathers. Ask God to show you how this reality is affecting your life today.

1 2 Sam 12:1–10

restorative justice

In the last year, who has offended you the most? How did you respond to the frustration and hurt it caused you?

1 Kings 1:28-53

d avid understood that in politics the incumbent has the advantage, and he knew how to use it. After hearing the report of Adonijah's treason, the aging king unleashed a media blitz of his own, loaning Solomon the royal 'limo,' publicly announcing him as the new king and placing him on the royal throne. David made sure Adonijah was out of the headlines for good. But behind these political fireworks are two important questions for us today. First, was David right to manipulate the situation as he did? After all, if Solomon was God's choice, shouldn't David have shown more trust, just 'let go and let God'? But trusting God doesn't mean we shouldn't take action. David's life and many other passages of Scripture demonstrate that faith and action, even bold action at times, can go together.[1] That doesn't mean everything we do is God's will – David's life is proof of this. But God does use our abilities and initiative to accomplish his purposes when our hearts are committed to listening to him and following his ways.

The second question in this drama is this: was Solomon wrong not to punish Adonijah? Don't we have the right to react when people do us wrong, for example if our spouse is unfaithful, our business partner cheats us or our ministry colleague betrays us? Yes, but the intent behind our response is all important. Note that Solomon didn't try to get even with Adonijah – he didn't show the lust for revenge that lies behind many of the world's current conflicts. Instead, he responded with 'restorative justice,' a combination of grace and firm standards (vs 52,53). That's a 'more excellent way'[2] to respond to personal and corporate injustice.

'Lord, I thank you for your restorative justice, shown to me over and over again. Reveal to me how I can bring your grace and standards to broken relationships in my life.'

[1] James 2:17 [2] 1 Cor 12:31b, AV

the secret of success

If you knew you were going to die today, what would you say to the people closest to you?

1 Kings 2:1-25

after forty years as king, David has a deathbed opportunity to pass on the secrets of his success to Solomon. An important ministry for older Christians is this building of relationships and sharing of the wisdom and experience gained over the years. Many young people today are hungry for such input. But the question here is, was David offering his son good advice or was he trying to manipulate the new king?

David's advice had two main themes. First, 'Be strong, show yourself a man' (v 2). Perhaps David thought a good leader needed a tough-guy image. But it's more likely that he was trying to prepare Solomon for the challenges to his authority that were just around the corner (vs 13–46). The second theme in David's advice, and certainly the secret to spiritual leadership, involved obedience: 'Observe what the LORD your God requires…' (v 3). Without that, even the strongest leader is doomed from the start. As it turned out, David's concern was well-founded. Adonijah's request to marry David's companion was yet another attempt to position himself as king. Solomon's patience with his older brother had run out and he moves to eliminate the problem for good. Solomon had learned that effective leadership sometimes requires strong, even unpleasant, action. It's interesting that Solomon already seems to have exhibited the gift of wisdom (vs 6,9). But God would soon transform this natural ability in the most wonderful way. In the end, Solomon was able to establish his throne (v 12) partly because he had natural ability and a good role model. But the most important thing was that God had chosen him and Solomon was willing to obey. Ultimately that's the secret of success.

What natural abilities has God given you? Spend some time praying about how you can use them for his purposes and then ask him to empower you with his Spirit so you can.

no more mister nice guy

Judgement is the natural consequence of our failure to respond to God's mercy.

1 Kings 2:26-46

W hat's gotten into Solomon? After beginning his reign with an impressive show of mercy (1:52,53), he enages in a ruthless 'clear-out' of his courtiers. By the end of this chapter, Adonijah, Abiathar, Joab and Shimei are all gone and the kingdom is 'firmly established in [his] hands' (v 46). Has power already corrupted King Solomon as it had King Saul?

Not at all. Solomon's case-by-case handling of each opponent shows he is becoming a wise leader, not a power-mad tyrant. Abiathar deserved death for his part in Adonijah's treason (v 26), but Solomon commuted his sentence because he had supported David in his hour of need,[1] and, most of all, because he was a priest of the Lord. Instead, Solomon fires him. Sometimes being removed from a position, although painful, can teach us an important lesson and give us a chance to start over somewhere else. But to benefit from such a 'severe mercy' we must avoid bitterness and ask, 'Lord, what are trying to teach me through this?' Joab also shared in David's hardships but he was guilty of murder and conspiracy, crimes that brought a death sentence (v 29). Shimei deserved punishment as well, but Solomon resisted the temptation to be vengeful (vs 8,9) and instead sentenced him to house arrest, an opportunity Shimei later squandered (vs 43–46). Watching loved ones make bad choices is incredibly painful. But we can trust that God is at work even when the situation seems hopeless.[2] We don't have the power of life or death in our dealings with others today, but our decisions can have a significant effect on them, for example, with difficult colleagues or wayward children. Like Solomon, we must always seek and use God's wisdom and opt for mercy whenever possible.

Is someone close to you making bad or destructive choices? Pray that God would show them his 'severe mercy', and that they would respond positively when he does.

[1] 1 Sam 23:6–13 [2] Ps 31:9–20

are you there, Lord?

What image or aspect of God is on your mind as you approach him today?

 Psalm 28

turning to prayer often initially brings out our anxious fears, rather than calming them. This psalm begins with the fear that prayer is all one way, like talking to someone who is deaf or deliberately ignoring us. The psalmist feels, almost literally, a 'dead loss'. He fears God is condemning him, lumping him in with the wicked. He feels anxiety that good and evil are so mixed in people and appearances can be so deceptive. So he longs to be reassured that his vision of a godly life is right; that corrupt and malicious people, who do not acknowledge and trust in God, will not ultimately flourish.

Putting our fears into words can often clear the ground. No reassurance is actually given, but the second half of the psalm expresses faith that God is, in fact, listening and can be trusted. The three images he uses for God in verses 7–9 are so familiar from the psalms and songs we sing in worship that they may easily lose their impact. Here they represent a progression of thought, appropriate for a Sunday.

A shield[1] is a close personal possession. It speaks of a God who graciously allows us to reach out and place him protectively between ourselves and the dangers we fear. A fortress is a large and strong place of communal safety. We enter it with others for times of fellowship and recuperation. Then we disperse again into the daily routine of the coming week with our own personal concerns, but can also carry in our hearts a sense of being together with others in a flock with the shepherd walking alongside, carrying individuals in times of greatest need.[2]

We need space for our questions, doubts and fears to surface in times and places where we also encounter reminders of the strength and mercy of the Lord.

1 Gen 15:1 2 Isa 40:11

two choices

Natural abilities empowered by the Spirit produce supernatural results. In prayer, reconsecrate your talents to God's service.

1 Kings 3:1-28

S o here we have it: Solomon's famous request for wisdom (v 9). If God gave me such an opportunity, I'd like to think that I'd ask for something similarly noble. But I'm not sure. What would you ask for?

It may seem like Solomon asked for wisdom 'out of the blue', that he had a spasm of clear thinking, just in time. But as we've seen, Solomon already had a gift for wisdom and he had been carefully cultivating and using it. Through the dream, God empowered Solomon's natural ability to a supernatural degree, which he immediately used to solve the conflict between the two prostitutes (vs 16–28). We all have God-given talents and the responsibility to use them for his glory.[1] But our natural abilities alone will fall short unless we offer them to God and ask his Spirit to empower us.

But in the midst of all the divine accolades for Solomon's wise request, it would be easy to overlook a second choice he made, one which is captured in a single word: 'except' (v 3). Solomon was committed to following the Lord, except for compromising with potential idolatry.[2] No big deal? Hardly! Solomon opened the door, ever so slightly, to a sin that would eventually destroy his nation.

That's how sin works. It doesn't seem like such a big deal at first. But it grows and grows until it finally takes over and destroys us.[3] The best strategy for avoiding the consequences of sin is to slam the door on it right away, even if people accuse us of being prudish or extreme. In the end, that's the wisest choice we can make.

Are there any 'excepts' in your walk with God? Ask God to show you what he wants you to do in these areas of your life.

[1] **Matt 25:14–30** [2] **1 Sam 9:12,13; Deut 12:2,3,13,14** [3] **Gal 6:7,8**

renaissance man

'The one who dies with the most toys wins.' Of course, as Christians we don't believe that. But how do we act?

1 Kings 4:20-34

Solomon had it all: wisdom, riches and fame. As a result, the people of Israel enjoyed an unprecedented time of peace and prosperity: 'They ate, they drank and they were happy' (v 20). Sounds good to me. Our passage emphasises two aspects of Solomon's wisdom. First, it was greater than any other. Because of God's empowerment, Solomon became the wisest man that ever lived (3:12), a fact that makes the book of Proverbs all the more fascinating. But secondly, we get a picture of the breadth of his understanding (v 29). Solomon was also a writer, a speaker, a composer and a naturalist (vs 32–34). Sometimes Christians can become one-dimensional, knowing almost everything about the Bible and almost nothing about the world. But in Solomon we get a vision for the well-rounded person of faith. Developing a zest for life and learning is contagious, and can only enhance our witness for Christ.

But for all his spectacular wisdom, the dark clouds of idolatry were beginning to gather on Solomon's horizon. It's worth pondering, especially for those of us who live in relative abundance, whether Israel's prosperity produced a spiritual laxness, or whether spiritual erosion undercut the peace and prosperity God had given them to enjoy. The way to avoid either trap is a renewed commitment to living disciplined, holy lives.[1] Solomon had yet to complete his crowning achievements – building God's temple and constructing his own palace. But they would be built on a weakened foundation (3:3). The only way to repair such damage is to repent, and commit ourselves to following God's ways, no matter what. But that's a difficult thing for wealthy and talented people to do.

Does your life reflect a balance between a zest for life and learning and a commitment to holy living? Which side of the equation needs development?

[1] 1 Pet 1:13–16

taking it further

key themes for study
Leadership. Whitney Kuniholm investigates the decisions each king made 'under all kinds of pressure – family jealousy, military attacks, political manoeuvring and the ever-present temptation to worship idols.' Frequently these pressures led the leaders of God's people to make rash decisions and to forget godly priorities.

Power. The handing over of power from David to Solomon did not go smoothly. Though sex could no longer stir David, a threat to his political plans certainly did! He reacts to Adonijah's challenge with decisiveness and skill. The Lord's will is accomplished (1:17,29,30,36,37,48), but it takes determined action from Nathan, Bathsheba, Benaiah and David for this to happen.

for reflection/discussion
What do you think of 'restorative justice' as a concept? Do you see 'a combination of grace and firm standards' best working as a response to injustice in personal relationships, as part of the criminal justice system or as a tool for reconciliation between alienated ethnic groups?

'Why are we so willing to compromise with sin, even though we know the consequences?' Do you think it is mainly because we 'are afraid to be seen as different', as Whitney Kuniholm suggests, or are there other reasons which are equally important?

for specific application
'By the end of his reign, Solomon seems to have been tempted by the trappings of his own success.' Have you been subtly changed in your values by increasing prosperity and influence? If so, what can you do about it?

'David's life and many other passages of Scripture demonstrate that faith and action, even bold action at times, can go together.' Is there any bold action, any dramatic initiative, you need to undertake in a spirit of faith?

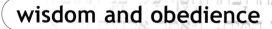

wisdom and obedience

as we launch into 1 Kings 5–11 we need to take a deep breath for the long haul (especially for the details of the Temple's construction in chapters 5–7) and arm ourselves with assurances such as Romans 15:4: 'For whatever was written in former days was written for our instruction, so that by steadfastness and by the encouragement of the scriptures we might have hope' (NRSV). Personally, I have been deeply instructed and greatly encouraged by the little-known author (at least to me) Dale Ralph Davis, whose commentary on 1 Kings, *The Wisdom and Folly*,[1] is a gold mine of spiritual truth and practical application.

So, as you read these 'God-breathed'[2] chapters, prepare to be instructed. Secondly, prepare to be astounded. Solomon's Temple was not one of the Seven Wonders of the World, but it must have come close. Look for the time and care lavished on the Temple and ask what this teaches us about our wonderful God. And all that gold – tons of it! How does this show his worth, his splendour, and the glory that is due to his name? Thirdly, prepare to be enlightened. There is so much in chapters 8–11 about God's character, his faithfulness and his expectations of us, his covenant people. Finally, prepare to be shocked. It is one of the most bewildering truths of Scripture that Solomon could be so wise, so blessed by God, but could ultimately depart from following him. What an exposé of the perversion of the human heart, my heart! Let's pray with Solomon:

'May the LORD our God be with us as he was with our fathers; may he never leave us nor forsake us. May he turn our hearts to him, to walk in all his ways and to keep the commands, decrees and regulations he gave our fathers' (8:57,58).

Ross Pilkinton

1 Christian Focus, 2002 2 2 Tim 3:16

rest and build

'Unless the LORD builds the house, its builders labour in vain.'[1]
As you enter God's presence, ask him to use you today.

1 Kings 5:1-6:10

When our boys were young, holidays were spent hiking in the mountains and forests of New Zealand. Living in huts and tents was exciting and challenging, but after some weeks, home had never seemed so good! In this passage, God declares to Israel that after 480 years of wandering they have at last arrived 'home' (5:3,4). This time of rest had been promised to David,[2] and included a place for settlement, freedom from disturbance and oppression, and lasting peace. Indeed, the important chronological verse 6:1 implies three historical periods – an era of slavery, an era of wandering, and now an era of rest. But paradoxically, this brief era of rest was to be a time for activity, a time to build.[3] The next three chapters are dominated by the exercise of Solomon's wise organisational skills, which was only possible because Israel entered such a time of rest. Eras of rest are granted by God,[4] and recent world events suggest that these may be coming to an end in many countries which have historically known the freedom of the gospel.

I write these notes in war-torn Nepal, where storm clouds of persecution once again threaten the church. Prior to 1990, many pastors and leading Christians were imprisoned for their faith, but with the arrival of democracy and the 'rest' it brought, the church has seen extraordinary growth. Westerners perhaps tend to think that rest is for personal development, enjoyment and even sleep. In Nepal it has been a time for building. 'Night is coming, when no one can work,' said Jesus.[5] How diligently are we using our times of rest or respite to build God's kingdom?

'But each one should build with care.'[6] How can you and your church take more seriously your responsibility to build the kingdom? How can you be better builders?

[1] Ps 127:1 [2] 2 Sam 7:10 [3] Eccl 3:3 [4] 1 Chr 22:9,10 [5] John 9:4 [6] 1 Cor 3:10

gold for God

God forbid that I should offer to God that which costs me nothing.1 Come into his presence and offer yourself today.

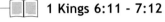

1 Kings 6:11 - 7:12

Solomon now turns to the construction of the interior of the Temple (6:15). Meanwhile, it is interesting to note that although contemporary building sites can be renowned for noise and bawdiness, the work on Solomon's Temple was so sacred that not even the sound of a hammer was heard (6:7). Perhaps the construction proceeded in total silence.2 We can only imagine the beauty and the grandeur of the finished structure. It is astounding that all the beautiful construction work in wood and stone was totally hidden, covered by a liberal overlay of the finest gold so that only God saw the quality of the underlying workmanship. The walls of the sanctuary and the main hall were covered with gold (6:20–22), as was the altar (6:22b), the cherubim (6:28), the doors (6:32,34), all the intricate ornamental carvings (6:35), and even the Temple floor (6:30). So much gold in God's Temple – we cannot even begin to imagine the value of such grandeur.

My wife and I were missionaries for several years in a poor community in the Philippines. Like the disciples we would be tempted to ask, 'Why this waste? … This perfume [or gold] could have been sold at a high price and the money given to the poor'.3 But as later chapters will show, God accepted Solomon's dedicated and costly workmanship. In all our Christian service there must be a place for lavish, exuberant, joyous gifts of gratitude to the Lord for all his goodness to us.4 However, we constantly need to remind ourselves that it is not our gifts that earn acceptance with him, be they ever so valuable, but our obedience to his will and our trust in his word (6:12,13).

What are some of the most valuable things in your life? Is there some way you can offer these back to God or share them with his people?

1 See 1 Chr 21:24 2 See Hab 2:20 3 Matt 26:8,9 4 John 12:1–8

our best for God

'I am the LORD your God; consecrate yourselves and be holy, because I am holy.'1 Consider your holiness in the light of his.

1 Kings 7:13-51

my father was a general engineer, and when I was a boy he sometimes took me to a foundry where large metal articles were being cast. I was fascinated by the skill of the foundrymen. I had to shade my eyes as they poured red-hot molten bronze or brass into carefully prepared sand moulds which later were prised apart, and behold – a bell, a bearing, or a bracket for my father's machines, although much detailed finishing work still had to be done. Huram had perfected the skill of casting bronze to a very high degree (v 14). But look at 2 Chronicles 2:13,14 to see his other remarkable abilities, and compare him with Bezalel and Oholiab, who, 'filled … with the Spirit of God',2 constructed the sanctuary and the tabernacle in the desert at Moses' direction. God wants our best – workmanship which shows his Spirit at work – whether we are a blacksmith, someone in a call centre, a lawyer or a pastry chef.

Throughout all of today's passage the writer finds obvious delight in describing the care, and the beauty of workmanship, lavished on the Temple furniture and implements (although 3,000 years later, we may struggle to understand their use). This is a model for how carefully and gladly we should seek to build our 'temples' – the temple of the church, and the temple of our bodies.3 With respect to the church, our building assignment is to labour with Christ 'to present her to himself as a radiant church, without stain or wrinkle or any other blemish, but holy and blameless.'4 With respect to ourselves, our assignment is to be holy as he is holy.5

Take time to wait upon God to ask how you can build up the 'temples' of your church and your own body. Share your findings with some trusted friends.

1 Lev 11:44 2 Exod 35:30–35 3 1 Cor 3:16; 6:19 4 Eph 5:27 5 1 Pet 1:13–16

the great Promise-keeper

'My eyes stay open through the watches of the night, that I may meditate on your promises.'[1] Meditate on his promises today.

1 Kings 8:1-21

imagine what the events of verses 10–13 meant to Solomon. The glory comes, the presence falls, God inhabits his Temple. I wonder if Solomon ever doubted whether it would happen? In our day the completion of the Temple would be a media spectacular – seven years in the building, no expense spared, the finest materials and craftsmanship, hundreds of thousands involved. The day was chosen (v 2), all Israel had gathered (v 14), the sacred tokens transferred (v 3), thousands of sacrifices made (v 5). But, what if God had not turned up? What if, after all the festivities – nothing?

Thankfully, 'when the priests withdrew from the Holy Place, the cloud filled the Temple of the LORD … for the glory of the LORD filled his Temple' (vs 10,11). What saved Solomon's Temple from becoming an immaculately crafted, exorbitantly expensive white elephant was the promise of God. Ten times in these prayers, Solomon declares that God is acting according to his covenant promises in building the Temple, establishing David's dynasty and abiding amongst his people (8:15 – 9:5). His promises, like his word, cannot be broken.[2] In 1936 God promised two British women they would 'take possession' of 'a land of mountains and valleys … a land the LORD your God cares for.'[3] They believed that land was Nepal, then closed to all foreigners. For 16 years they prayed on the Indian border believing God would fulfil his promise. In 1952 permission was finally given and they entered Nepal to begin a remarkable medical missionary work, especially serving leprosy sufferers in western Nepal. In these days when promises are so easily made and broken, how wonderful it is that we have a promise-keeping God!

Recall some of God's promises that have been important in your life. Thank him for those fulfilled, trust him for those to come.

1 Ps 119:148 2 John 10:35b 3 Deut 11:11,12

fearful yet majestic God

What does the weather map of human affairs look like today?
Bring to God any news headlines buzzing in your mind.

Psalm 29

On a sunny day, looking out on a calm landscape, cultivated and domesticated by human efforts, it is easy to feel we are masters of our life and destiny. When a storm comes, we may be thrilled by the magnificence of lightning and energised by rumbling thunder, but we are right to be afraid. Despite all our technology, we are powerless before a wind that tears off roofs and fells trees, or rain that swells rivers into floods!

The original singers of this psalm will have seen many dramatic storms sweep in from the sea and extend across their land from northern forests (v 5) to southern deserts (v 8). In pagan myths, elements in nature are identified with particular gods and define their character; thunder is usually the voice of a powerful, unpredictable god. In the Hebrew Scriptures all of creation together points to the Creator but God is not defined by any one of its themes. He is like the white light that comes when the colours of the spectrum shine together.

So the psalm begins with the glory, strength and splendour, acknowledged at all times by choruses of angels ('mighty ones', v 1), deserving human wonder and praise. Then it picks out the colours of judgement and salvation. It reminds us that, at any moment, the voice of the Lord can break through into human affairs like a storm, washing away debris, blowing down decaying structures and leaving behind plentiful water and the peace in which new life can flourish. The commentator Kidner points out that the word for 'flood' (v 10) is found only in the story of Noah,[1] an early picture of how God's judgement and salvation fit together.

In modern cultures people easily panic when events seem disastrous. God's people can be active in the clear up, but also calm in trusting that God's winds blow for good.[2]

[1] Gen 6–10; Kidner, Psalms 1–72, IVP [2] Rom 8:28

immense but accessible

'I live in a high and holy place, but also with him who is contrite and lowly in spirit.'[1] 'O God, live in me today.'

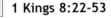

1 Kings 8:22-53

d addy, where does God live?', asked little Suzy, just home from junior church. 'God lives everywhere,' replied her orthodox father. Lifting his empty coffee cup from the table she continued, 'Well, is he in this cup?' 'I suppose he must be in the cup!' replied her father. 'Got him!', shouted the little girl triumphantly covering the rim with her hand.

This simple but profound story illustrates the theology behind verses 27–30 of today's passage. On Saturday, we read Solomon's claim to have built 'a place for you to dwell for ever' (v 13). Now he confesses, 'The heavens, even the highest heaven, cannot contain you. How much less this Temple I have built!' (v 27). God is immense in his majesty yet confined in his accessibility. He dwells in the highest heaven, yet in a Temple made by human hands. The first shows his transcendence, the second his availability. Indeed, do we not get a glimpse here of that greatest of all biblical paradoxes, the incarnation?[2]

One of the great benefits of God's availability is that we can bring our petitions to him; one of the great benefits of his transcendence is that he can do something about them. So Solomon presents seven great prayer scenarios (vs 32–49), each echoing the cry of verse 30b: 'Hear from heaven, your dwelling-place, and when you hear, forgive'. Note the gravity of these prayer situations, dealing with crises like drought, famine, siege, war and captivity. In these troubled days we very much need to learn that our freely accessible God is powerful to answer the big prayers as well as the small.[3]

Praise God that he is immense but accessible. Bring your 'big' prayers to him today. Include prayers for justice, peace and righteousness in the world.

[1] Isa 57:15 [2] John 1:14 [3] Luke 18:7,8

a bouquet of blessing

'Praise be to the God and Father of our Lord Jesus Christ, who has blessed us … with every spiritual blessing in Christ.'[1]

1 Kings 8:54-66

t he fervour of Solomon's thanksgiving and intercession has driven him to his knees (v 54 – compare v 22), but now he stands to give a prayer of blessing to 'the whole assembly of Israel' (v 55). In your prayers for your family, friends and colleagues do you sometimes struggle, as I do, to get beyond immediate needs, to their spiritual well-being? In today's passage, Solomon gives us a model of how to pray for spiritual blessing for God's people.[2] He begins by praising the Lord for the kind of God he is, that he is faithful to all his many promises (v 56). Then he asks that God's people will know his abiding presence – as God has been with them in the past, may they know his presence in the future (v 57). Next he asks that God will keep their hearts faithful and their actions obedient (v 58). He then asks that they will have God's spiritual and material provision for 'each day's need' (v 59). Finally, he prays that their lives will proclaim that the Lord alone is God and that they are committed only to him (vs 60,61).

I am writing this note on the 34th birthday of my third son. I could not be present at his birth, so to convey my gratitude and love I sent my wife a huge bouquet of spring flowers. Praying a prayer like Solomon's each day for our loved ones is like giving them a bouquet of blessings, which will bring a beauty and fragrance into their lives that will last into eternity. No wonder the passage finishes with a huge party and they 'went home joyful and glad in heart' (vs 65,66)!

To give more reality to your intercession for a family member, friend or colleague, pray through Ephesians 1:15-19 with their name inserted instead of 'you' and 'your'.

1 Eph 1:3 **2 See** Num 6:24-26; Eph 1:15–23

Mr Wiseman, beware!

Ponder this today: 'The fear of the LORD is the beginning of wisdom, and knowledge of the Holy One is understanding'.1

1 Kings 9:1-28

S olomon was an inveterate builder and nine times in this diverse chapter various building schemes are mentioned. They include the Temple and royal palace (vs 1,3), the palace of Pharaoh's daughter (v 24), numerous cities and walls (vs 15–19) and a fleet of ships to transport gold from his celebrated mines (vs 26–28). But in a second supernatural appearance (see 3:4–15), God warns Solomon that all will disintegrate to dust and ashes if he does not remain faithful (vs 4–9). One commentator summarises the high cost of Solomon's apostasy as 'the loss of turf, Temple and throne' (Dale R Davis). In those heady days of empire-building it must have seemed inconceivable that Solomon and his fabulous Temple could become an object of ridicule and scorn to the surrounding nations (vs 7,8). But we know the end of the story – the inconceivable happened, disaster fell because of the disobedience and idolatry of this astoundingly gifted and uniquely blessed leader of God's people. Verse 4 is the key: 'If you walk before me in integrity of heart and uprightness, as David your father did, and do all I command and observe my decrees and laws…' This obedience is crucial and foundational – it is loving the Lord our God with all the heart, soul, mind and strength.2 God calls us, alongside Solomon, to nothing less.

But we should not think that we can automatically avoid Solomon's apostasy. Recently, I heard of some early disciples in Nepal who suffered for their faith, even going to prison, but who are now no longer believers. A major theme of Scripture, particularly the book of Hebrews, is to warn believers about unbelief and apostasy.3 We need to take such warnings seriously.

Read Hebrews 3:12–15. Is there someone who is struggling whom you can encourage today? Can you visit them, help them in some way, pray with them?

1 Prov 9:10 2 Mark 12:29–30 3 Heb 6:1–8; 10:26–31

Solomon, super-king

'But remember the LORD your God, for it is he who gives you the ability to produce wealth.'[1] Thank him now for all you have.

1 Kings 10:1-29

here is Solomon in all his glory.[2] The writer of 1 Kings seems to struggle to adequately express Solomon's magnificence. Instead, we find expressions like 'far exceeded' (v 7), 'never again' (v 10), or 'nothing like it' (v 20). Verse 23 is another such eulogy for a super-king: 'King Solomon was greater in riches and wisdom than all the other kings of the earth'.

So what are we to make of it all? First, we need to put from our minds the knowledge that Solomon's crash is coming and simply rejoice in the wonder of God's beneficence to one of his chosen servants. Riches, wisdom, craftsmanship, organisational skill and the administration of justice and righteousness are all gifts from God that need to be acknowledged and esteemed. God loves the rich as much as the poor[3] – a truth those of us committed to serving the poor constantly need to keep before us.

Secondly, we catch here a picture of the coming kingdom of God. The Queen of Sheba and the multitudes suggested by verses 24 and 25 prefigure the great company of nations flowing into God's kingdom of wisdom, justice, righteousness and plenty.[4] The Queen of Sheba was not Jewish (Sheba was probably in modern-day Yemen). Praise God that she pointed the way to the kingdom for us Gentiles today. Thirdly, there is a warning here. The Queen of Sheba responded in wonder, perhaps even in faith (v 5,9) at the splendour of Solomon. Jesus was far greater than Solomon, yet the leaders of his day spurned him.[5] May there be no such root of unbelief in us.

Do you think there are areas of unbelief in your life? Commit these to the Lord and ask for help to trust him more deeply.

[1] **Deut 8:18** [2] **Matt 6:29** [3] **Mark 10:21–22** [4] **Mic 4:1–4** [5] **Matt 12:42**

take time to tremble

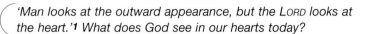

'Man looks at the outward appearance, but the LORD looks at the heart.'[1] What does God see in our hearts today?

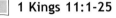

1 Kings 11:1-25

f inally, the crash comes! 'Solomon did evil in the eyes of the LORD; he did not follow the LORD completely, as David his father had done' (v 6). Outwardly Solomon's sin was marrying pagan women,[2] but inwardly it was embracing other gods besides the Lord (v 4). Our God will tolerate no rivals. Like a faithful husband, God demonstrates holy anger when his people break the sanctity of their covenant relationship by giving themselves to another (v 9). Solomon must suffer the consequences of this disobeying the first commandment – the raising up of 'adversaries' Hadad, Rezon and Jeroboam (vs 14,23,26).

Notice how the word 'heart' is used in verses 2–4. To the Hebrews 'the heart' meant the mind and will as well as the emotions, the totality of the inner life. Solomon's heart – his inner person, had turned after other gods (v 4). Long before he built Chemosh chapel or Molech meeting house for his wives (v 7), Solomon had began the inward descent into compromise and permissiveness. With me, do you find this a little frightening? After all the wisdom and wealth God had lavished upon Solomon, even appearing to him on two occasions in epiphanies (v 9; 3:5; 9:2), Solomon fell at the end of his life (v 4).

Revelation's warning to the church at Ephesus seems appropriate: 'I know your deeds, your hard work and your perseverance … Yet I hold this against you: You have forsaken your first love'.[3] With sadness I recall several former ministerial and missionary colleagues who are no longer walking with the Lord. We need to take time to tremble, to see if perhaps our love has grown cold, and if so, to seek repentance.[4]

Take time to tremble. Remember God's exclusive claim to our worship, love and service. Renew your commitment to him today.

[1] 1 Sam 16:7 **[2]** Exod 34:11–16 **[3]** Rev 2:2–4 **[4]** Rev 2:5

discerning the big picture

'For God is the King of all the earth; sing to him a psalm of praise.'1 Joyfully acknowledge his sovereign rule today.

1 Kings 11:26-43

S olomon and his dynasty are coming to an end (v 43). Israel's golden age of influence, prosperity and peace is over, shattered by Solomon's disobedience of the covenant obligations (vs 31–33). Using graphic, prophetic drama, Ahijah demonstrates how the unified kingdom is to be torn in pieces and the major portion given to Jeroboam, one of Solomon's administrators (vs 28–31). Three times in yesterday's reading the writer of 1 Kings used this tearing imagery which seems particularly appropriate to show the calamity about to devastate Solomon's kingdom (vs 11,12,13).

I have called this note 'Discerning the big picture' because behind the rise and fall of the motley collection of kings (and queens) who will follow Solomon, God is at work. History is his story. Solomon disobeys God, Rehoboam institutes depraved worship (14:24) and Jeroboam becomes a paradigm for evil (16:2), yet God is still in control (v 31,32). Even in today's passage, in verse 39 there is a ray of hope: 'I will humble David's descendants … but not for ever'. From the family of David, Solomon and Rehoboam will come 'Jesus, who is called Christ'.2 In these turbulent days Christians need to resolutely embrace the truth and remember the assurance that history is God's and he is working his purpose out, as year succeeds to year.3 As I write this note there are reports of yet another 100 people killed in the Maoist insurgency that is raging throughout this land, where some years ago ten members of the Nepali royal family were exterminated by one of their own. But we have to believe God is still in control; our urgent task is to discern how he is working out his purposes.4

Can you (or others you know) discern any 'signs of the times' relevant to your country and church just now? Do not exclude the possibility of signs of judgement.

1 Ps 47:7 2 Matt 1:6,7,16 3 Dan 2:21 4 Matt 16:3

taking it further

key themes for study

The Temple. Ross Pilkinton speaks of 'the obvious delight the writer finds in describing the care and the beauty of the workmanship lavished on the Temple furniture and implements.' Such work demonstrates the work of the Spirit. The New Testament teaches us to look forward to a renewed creation, and the holy city into which 'the glory and honour of the nations' will be brought.[1] Nothing lovely will be wasted or lost!

God's covenant faithfulness. Throughout these chapters there is a stress on God's fulfilment of his promises to David (for example 5:5,7; 6:12; 7:51; 9:4,5; 11:12). God's 'faithful love promised to David'[2] is later seen as the model for the 'everlasting covenant' God makes with all who trust in him.

Apostasy. Solomon's deliberate refusal to keep the Lord's commands, although he 'had appeared to him twice' (11:9; 3:5), is a warning to us all. A good start is no guarantee of a good finish. We may think too of Judas,[3] or Phygelus, Hermogenes and Demas.[4]

for reflection/discussion

May the Lord our God uphold 'the cause of his people Israel according to each day's need, so that all the peoples of the earth may know that the LORD is God and that there is no other.' (1 Kings 8:59b,60).

'We have to believe God is still in control; our urgent task is to discern how he is working out his purposes.' Do you agree that such discernment is our duty? If so, how should we go about it?

for specific application

'In all our Christian service there must be a place for ... joyous gifts of gratitude to the Lord for all his goodness to us', but above all we need to demonstrate 'our obedience to his will and our trust in his word.' What does this say to you right now?

[1] Rev 21:26 [2] Isa 55:3 [3] John 13:2,27 [4] 2 Tim 1:15; 4:10

Ross Pilkinton

following his footsteps

as a teenager, Moses' words in Exodus 4:10 were heavily underscored in my Bible: 'O LORD, I have never been eloquent, neither in the past nor since you have spoken to your servant. I am slow of speech and tongue.' I spent my early years avoiding speaking in public except on the playing field where I was particularly voluble, probably because sport was the one area where I excelled. I recall one painful incident when I was twelve years old and my turn came to give a 'morning talk' in front of my classmates. As I began to speak, the zealous teacher plucked the notes from my hand and the big sports hero collapsed in tears and ran from the classroom in humiliation.

My hero was my eldest brother, ten years my senior, who became a Christian in the wave of new life that swept New Zealand churches in the years following World War II. When he left home to become a missionary carpenter in Vanuatu (then New Hebrides), I missed him terribly. Wanting to follow in his footsteps, I became a Christian at a young people's Easter camp when I was fifteen years old. Romans 10:9 was important in my conversion. I knew I believed, but the verse also said, 'Confess with your mouth, "Jesus is Lord"'. Oh dear, how could I possibly do that?

It was not the kind of camp where commitments were openly acknowledged, but on that Easter Monday morning I stood and testified to my new-found faith anyway. Then an amazing thing happened: for the first time I sensed a boldness, an assurance, a profound fulfilment in speaking publicly about Jesus Christ, a sense that has rarely left me these last fifty years.

After secondary school I began training as an electrical engineer, but each time I spoke in youth groups or churches (albeit still

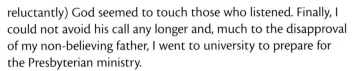

reluctantly) God seemed to touch those who listened. Finally, I could not avoid his call any longer and, much to the disapproval of my non-believing father, I went to university to prepare for the Presbyterian ministry.

Since then my wife and I have served in several churches of various denominations, in youth organisations and as an industrial chaplain. Our many years with Scripture Union, working in churches and schools, were especially fruitful and fulfilling.

But slowly God was turning our hearts towards the poor. Study of the Scriptures and raising four sons in a working class, multicultural suburb helped, as did books like Ronald Sider's *Rich Christians in an age of hunger* (Hodder and Stoughton), plus the example of other believers simplifying their lives in response to the challenge of world poverty.

Finally, when our family had grown up, God called us to serve the poor more directly. We joined a little-known mission group called Servants to Asia's Urban Poor and lived for several years in a poor community in Metro Manila. More recently, we have served in Nepal with the International Nepal Fellowship, caring for fellow missionaries who are seeking to serve the poor and marginalised.

How good God has been to us, and how much he has taught us, especially through living amongst poor people. Once we were robbed, and everything that could be carried or sold was taken. The next day a poor man we were trying to reach came to us and said, 'Now we can be friends, for you have suffered as we suffer'. Suffering with others opens many doors, a truth we should have known from the example of our Saviour.

We have much yet to learn on our journey, but Psalm 84:5 encourages us: 'Blessed are those whose strength is in you, who have set their hearts on pilgrimage'.

dancing after danger

'God of mercy, God of grace, Show the brightness of your face.'

Psalm 30

t he obvious context for this psalm is the experience of someone who has been sick or wounded, feeling he was sinking down, close to death. Elizabeth Kübler-Ross studied terminal illness in the 1960s.[1] She described patients 'bargaining', like children making wheedling offers to be helpful or put something right, if only parents will grant what they desperately want. There are a number of examples in the Bible of people bargaining in prayer for their lives.[2] They can be read, not as evidence that God is easily manipulated, but as examples that we can bring to God raw, childish feelings along with our urgent requests and still be welcomed.

This psalmist's bargain was that, alive, his voice could still praise God and pass on the news of God's power to save (v 9). Having recovered, he is energetically fulfilling the promise he implied. Now that he is singing and dancing again, the dark days when God seemed withdrawn in anger appear like a brief overnight visit compared with a lifelong relationship with God's grace (v 5). There are hints that he has gained from his suffering. He has lost an unrealistic sense of security that nothing can shake him, but gained more trust that God can bring him through.

It may seem too personal a psalm to be set for a public festival dedicating the Temple. Some even suggest the heading belongs to the previous psalm.[3] Healing, however, especially from the threat of death, is one of the most pervasive biblical images for God's salvation. Every worshipping congregation can sing this song, connecting it with our own experiences of Easter joy.

If your life comes under threat, will the desire to live on to praise and proclaim Christ be genuinely on your bargaining list with God?

[1] *On Death and Dying* [2] Isa 38:3,18 [3] Compare Hab 3:19

בְּרֵאשִׁית בָּרָא אֱלֹהִים אֵת הַשָּׁמַיִם וְאֵת הָ
הָיְתָה תֹהוּ וָבֹהוּ וְחֹשֶׁךְ עַל־פְּנֵי תְהוֹם
עַל־פְּנֵי הַמָּיִם: וַיֹּאמֶר אֱלֹ

decline... and fall?

at the level of secular history, 1 Kings 12–16 deals with the disastrous but crucial period immediately following the reign of Solomon, from 930 to 874 BC. The most significant event of these years was the division of the old, intact Israel into two: the new northern kingdom of Israel, and the southern kingdom of Judah. This one incident was to influence the course of world history, for it created the Jews, who now occupy such a pivotal and influential position in world events. But this is not secular history. We miss the point if we read it that way, merely trying to align the account here with other historical accounts outside the Scriptures. The author was not primarily interested in secular but in religious history. He was neither precisely mapping the rise and fall of nations, nor detailing Israel's economic and political fortunes. Rather, he was charting the religious decline of the people of God, led by a succession of godless and self-seeking kings. These kings perpetuated and expanded the idolatry and associated immorality that had been introduced in the later years of Solomon's reign. There is a constant feeling here that even if it is a long time coming, disaster is inevitable. The challenge for us, faced with these otherwise depressing readings, is to struggle yet again with Scripture's most unfathomable paradox: the interrelationship between God's will and human freedom. Can the future be changed? Is history predetermined? Can God's judgement be avoided? Can God's blessings be lost? Does the fulfilment of prophecy depend upon human response? These questions have always troubled thoughtful people and no doubt always will, but it is the opportunity to grapple anew with such questions that makes these readings worth the effort.

further reading
Simon J DeVries, *1 Kings*, Word, 1985; Choon-Leong Seow, 'The First and Second Books of Kings', *The New Interpreter's Bible*, Volume 3, Abingdon Press.

John Harris

the heavy and light yokes

'Lord, I don't know what coming days may bring me, in choices or advice. How can I rely on you for everything?'

1 Kings 12:1-24

k ing succeeds king, but the crown was not on Rehoboam's head before his foolishness split the kingdom, fulfilling the judgement placed on his father, who had risked all to flirt with foreign gods. At least Solomon was remembered for wisdom in state matters. Rehoboam preferred 'the boys' (one possible Hebrew translation) over his father's wiser old advisers, opting for the foolish opinions of court hangers-on to inaugurate his disastrous kingship. We recognise Rehoboam in some modern national leaders and corporate bosses – ruthless, hard-line, ill-advised dictators. They consider complaints and dissatisfaction a threat to their position rather than opportunities for reconciliation, responding instead by abusing their power as if it is a force to be wielded 'harshly' (v 13). Rehoboam's response to his petitioners was vulgar as well as harsh – NIV 'little finger' is rather too genteel a euphemism for his precise meaning (v 10). Like most weak but authoritarian leaders, he already despised his own people. The consequences for himself and his kingdom are a stern warning to any who might be newly appointed to authority. Enthusiastic descriptions of Solomon's grandeur, and ostentatious wealth (10:14–29), mask the burden of taxes and public works which the people, particularly those remote from Jerusalem, were tired of bearing. Rehoboam's threat of an even heavier yoke contrasts starkly with Jesus' offer to the weary and burdened, of a yoke which is easy and a burden which is light.[1] Jesus specifically denounced a Rehoboam-like style of leadership,[2] and his words were remembered and echoed by Peter.[3] Yet he does offer a yoke, implying discipline as well as rest. Those who seek this rest must follow the path of service and humility.

'Take my yoke upon you and learn from me, for I am gentle and humble in heart and you will find rest for your souls'.[4]

1 Matt 11: 28–30 **2** Mark 10:42 **3** 1 Pet 5:2,3 **4** Matt 11:29

after the revolution

'O God, whose service is perfect freedom...' (the Book of Common Prayer*)*.

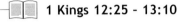

1 Kings 12:25 - 13:10

We readily sympathise with the oppressed northerners, glad that God is on their side (12:24). But it is no surprise that the rebel warlord turns out to be flawed. God's will is to liberate the oppressed, but this story warns us not to romanticise popular uprisings. Revolutionaries' courage and charisma does not always translate into wise and compassionate government. Many leaders have personal agendas, and scheme to retain popular support. So Jeroboam pays lipservice to a kind of liberation theology (a god 'who brought you up out of Egypt', v 28), but his loyalty is to himself. He probably did not intend to found a new religion but represented God by an ancient symbol, the Bull of Jacob (the Hebrew word for 'bull' is very similar to 'Mighty One').[1] Nevertheless, he contravened the Law[2] and his 'calves' eventually led to idolatry.[3]

The writer's scandalised feelings at Jeroboam's altar and assumption of priestly status show in the way he highlights the strange story of the man of God from Judah. Today, we see him at the height of his power – the channel of God's word, by which the altar was destroyed, and Jeroboam's arm shriveled and restored. Yet, like the rest of us, his real test will not be in confrontation with the king but in obedience in lesser things (13:8,9). Like this man of God, we may find within us the strength to respond to God and preach, heal or help lead someone to Christ. It is in the seemingly smaller matters that we fail. God demands a high standard of obedience from his people, particularly those he calls to special service.

The same God who calls us to be brave in confronting evil also calls us to obedience in the small things of life. What in your life is the Spirit putting his finger on now?

1 Gen 49:24; Ps 132:2, NIV **'Mighty One'** **2 Deut 12:5–7; 18:1–8** **3 Hos 10:5**

prophecy and failure

Before reading, let us pause first, to ask forgiveness from God for our failures.

1 Kings 13:11-34

W hy give so detailed an account of these two men of God? The answer lay 300 years ahead when Josiah finally destroyed the shrine at Bethel.[1] With such a distant goal, how was anyone to know if the man from Judah spoke for God? To destroy the altar and restore the king's hand was not enough. He had to bear in his own self the tokens of his calling. Only in publicly suffering for his seemingly minor disobedience could he show the truth of his proclamation. We might find it easy to identify with this man. Few of us are flagrant sinners like Jeroboam, or have the status to commit sins that affect a nation. We are ordinary, decent, faithful people who try to please God. But we can disobey in 'smaller' things. He is a warning to us that temptation comes from unexpected places and that we are most vulnerable after exceptional spiritual experiences. What about the old man of God from Bethel? We identify less with him because he seems so blatantly deceptive. Yet we are also capable of 'taking the name of God in vain',[2] claiming to have a 'word from the Lord' when we do not, or using the name of God to manipulate others. But we too, like the old prophet, can repent of our duplicity. In the end he recognised a real man of God and hoped to gain forgiveness by identifying with him in his death. Centuries later the resting place of the two men of God was the only tomb Josiah left standing.[1]

There has only ever been one sinless Man of God.[3] Like the man of God from Judah, he too was laid in someone else's tomb. And we, by identifying with him in his death, truly gain forgiveness of sin.

'If we have been united with him in his death, we will certainly also be united with him in his resurrection'.[4] Give thanks!

[1] **2 Kings 23:16–18** [2] **Exod 20:7, AV** [3] **1 Pet 3:18** [4] **Rom 6:5**

the death of a child

'Lord have mercy, Christ have mercy, Lord have mercy.'

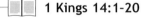

1 Kings 14:1-20

On a remote Vanuatu island, local Christians are translating the books of 1 and 2 Kings into their Raga language. Visiting them, I am humbled by their dedication but challenged by their questions. Today's reading posed particular problems – notably the puzzling Hebrew of verse 14b. There is also the vexed question of punctuation. When is Ahijah speaking and when is God? Has the writer inserted his own comments? Verses 10 and 11 are difficult because they are actually two rude little poems. By substituting 'male' for AV's 'him that pisseth against the wall', NIV perhaps prudishly sanitises an obvious crudity. Punctuating the 'clean' version as if God is speaking skirts the problem of God reciting obscenities. Crude insults are not uncommon in explicit biblical narratives but it is not just conservative modesty to suggest that they are more suited to someone such as Rabshakeh taunting Hezekiah[1] than they are to a holy God. No wonder many commentators propose a later editorial hand!

Bible scholars must never let struggles with the text blind them to God's voice speaking to all of us through it. This story shows that God remains in control, while people try to solve their problems for themselves. Jeroboam seeks the answer he wants by manipulating others – but God intervenes, thwarting his scheme. Yet even amid severe judgement, mercy is shown. Anyone whose children die innocently, caught up in the consequences of other's actions, should read this otherwise unpleasant story carefully. In the midst of it all, God has mercy on a child who is a victim of others' evil – a severe mercy, but we, knowing the power of the sacrificial death of Christ, may believe that God has taken this child-victim to himself.

'Lord, have mercy on all children who are victims, all who are abused, frightened, homeless or facing death. Lord, have mercy.'

[1] 2 Kings 18:27

grasp the moment or lose it

*'O God, open our hearts and minds to respond
to your Word today.'*

1 Kings 14:21-31

t he opposing kings both had sons named Abijah. Jeroboam's son died young, the innocent first casualty of his father's ambition and idolatry. Rehoboam's son lived to succeed his father, although Rehoboam was no more faithful to God than his northern rival. The difference was that while Jeroboam's descendants were the unfortunate victims of God's judgement on him, Rehoboam's descendants were the undeserving inheritors of God's favour to their ancestor David[1] and to Jerusalem (11:13). Rehoboam need not have perpetuated the idolatry and immoral practices foolishly permitted by his father. He could have led the nation back to God. He did not, but his own son succeeded him as king and a glimmer of hope remained – yet hope would not remain forever. God's promise was not one-sided. As the slow demise of the kings of Judah clearly shows, God's patience lasts a long time but eventually he requires a response. God's blessing finally rests only on those who receive it in faith, and allow it to fashion their lives.

We now know that God's eternal blessings to David are fulfilled in Jesus, the perfect Son of David[2] and that God's election of Jerusalem is ultimately fulfilled in the spiritual Jerusalem, the community of the people of God.[3] This blessing and election is not something we can take for granted. Rehoboam had an opportunity – which he rejected – to grasp the moment, to live a faithful life and thus to set an example of godliness to the kings he fathered. We too must grasp the moments we are given, accept the blessings which God offers us in Jesus, the Son of David, and strive to live a godly life and to be a blessing to others.

*'Take my life and let it be, consecrated Lord to thee …
Take my will and make it thine, it shall be no longer mine'.[4]*

[1] **2 Sam 7:16** [2] **Luke 1: 32,69** [3] **Heb12:22** [4] **FR Havergal, 1838–79**

godly scholarship

'O God, help us to sense your presence, active in history and active in our own lives.'

1 Kings 15:1-24

The author tersely dismisses the brief kingship of Abijah, but gives more details of Asa's rule. This is due both to Asa's religious reforms and his long reign (overlapping with seven northern kings) and collaboration with Syria.

We should always note the way authors select and use their sources. The author of 1 Kings made use of both oral history and existing documentary evidence (vs 7,23). Just as Jesus did far more than John could record,[1] so this writer had more material than he could use. Ancient historians tended to have a well-developed theory of history, carefully selecting their information to demonstrate that view. The writer of 1 Kings was no exception. His material is carefully chosen to support his view of history, made all the more obvious because the writer of Chronicles deals differently with the same era, using different sources to make different points. Thus in Chronicles Abijah is portrayed as defending Jerusalem and the Davidic line, while in 1 Kings he is dismissed as a worthless nonentity, perpetuating the idolatry of his father.[2] To the writer of 1 Kings, the history of both kingdoms was shaped by the disobedience of the kings. Corrupt rule eventually brought God's judgement, even if it was to be a defeat and exile long distant in the future. The occasional good kings could not slow the downward spiral beyond their own reigns. The Chronicles perspective, that obedience to the Law and respect for God's Temple at Jerusalem would have guaranteed the nation's future, was the other side of the same coin. The pattern was not hard to see, writing after the event, but for us the lesson is the same. Faithfulness and disobedience both have consequences beyond the span of our own lives.

'Grant us in this world knowledge of your truth, and in the world to come life everlasting'.[3]

[1] John 21:25 [2] 2 Chr 13 [3] John Chrysostom, c347–407

in God's hands

*Choosing a safe and comfortable place to pray can be a
helpful symbol when life is fraught with stress.*

Psalm 31

i n times of crisis it can be a relief to have someone we trust
to hug or hold us. In this psalm the safety and reassurance
God provides is expressed in metaphors about hands. In the
middle of danger, the psalmist places his inner life into God's
hands (v 5). He shudders at the thought of relying on a
substitute, an idol that is bound to let him down. Once firmly in
God's arms he will not be handed over to any enemy, but set
firmly down in a place where he can move safely again.

These comforting pictures lead him on to describe more vividly
how bad he really feels. He recognises that the causes of his
distress will not be swiftly resolved; much endurance will be
needed. So he pictures, not only his spirit here and now, but
also the whole span of his life across time, safely held in God's
hands (v 15).

There are vivid examples of this psalm being used by others in
the Bible. 'Terror on every side', was Jeremiah's experience as he
was beaten and persecuted. He too found that the thought of
being snatched by God from the hands of the wicked, led him
on to express his anguish more deeply.[1] And Jesus quotes from
this psalm in his final moments on the cross, committing
himself into God's hands for the journey into death.[2]

The apostle Paul saw needing to receive comfort at times as
inevitable for a Christian and the basis for being able to give it.
'As the sufferings of Christ flow over into our lives, so also
through Christ our comfort overflows'.[3]

*Don't rush the process of comforting people. Some long to
be with people who believe in God's comfort, yet want to
be permitted to say how hopeless they still really feel.*

[1] **Jer 20:10,13,14** [2] **Luke 23:46** [3] **2 Cor 1:4,5**

God's will, human responsibility

'How long, O LORD, how long?'[1]

1 Kings 15:25 - 16:14

t he author commences here a series of terse reports on successive northern kings. Despite much historical detail and indications of archival sources, the reports are not intended as objective accounts of these kings. The only measure of their performance is their godlessness, the degree to which they emulated Jeroboam.

An important subtext to this dry litany of bad kings is Scripture's most unfathomable paradox: the interplay of God's will and human responsibility. Just as God's blessing can be lost, his punishment can be averted. The fact that judgement on the house of Jeroboam was delayed long enough for his son to take the throne raised the faint possibility of hope for Israel. Nadab could have chosen God's way, changing the course of history. But he did not, and the narrator makes it clear that he paid for his own sins, not the sins of his father. Nadab's killer became king. Yet Baasha, despite God's judgement on Jeroboam's line, was not the instrument of God's will. His selfish destruction of Jeroboam's household is simply the same political violence we witness globally today. Being no better than Jeroboam, Baasha merited no dynasty. His family also fell victims to the prophetic judgement upon their father. Yet Baasha's son, Elah, died for his own sins, like Nadab and Baasha before him. Human beings may seem to be the main actors on the stage of history but they are not. God's will is still being played out. The passing of millennia must not blunt our sensitivity to God's purposes for his world. Whether we are national leaders or humble citizens, we all have the opportunity to align ourselves with God's will for his world. We ignore it at our peril.

'God is working his purpose out as year succeeds to year: God is working his purpose out and the time is drawing near.' **2**

1 Ps 6:3 **2** AC Ainger, hymn writer, 1841–1919

two parallel histories

To know the truth we need to hear God's story, not just the human story.

1 Kings 16:15-34

Little has altered since the time of these kings. Military coups, treason, revolutions, assassinations – change the names and dates and it's today's TV news. A rebel militia readily becomes a law unto itself. Zimri's insurrection angered the army (v 16). A quick military coup and General Omri is installed as king (v 22). Scholars often point out the apparent historical incompleteness of Kings. Extra-biblical sources show that Omri was a powerful leader, influencing neighbouring nations. But the author was not interested in Omri's political and military successes, relegating them to the ancient equivalent of a footnote (v 27) – he is interested in success only as God judges it. The strongest possible words of condemnation are reserved for Ahab. Judged by God's standards, he was even worse than the rest. The author makes it very clear that Ahab chose his own path (v 31).

Then, as now, two parallel histories are unfolding. One is secular history, from the human viewpoint; the other is the real, spiritual story, as God sees it. In the real history, leaders are not measured by popular success, but by their faithfulness to God's will. In these stories, reaching us across nearly 3,000 years, we are challenged to consider a history which transcends social, economic and political factors but is understood only with reference to the more lasting issues of faith and obedience. And beyond them, yet again, we glimpse the tension between God's eternal will and human free will arrogantly choosing its own destructive path. The choice that had to be made under the old covenant must still be faced under the new covenant. Guilt can be taken away by the shed blood of Jesus. God's righteous judgement can be averted. But still we must choose.

'The world and its desires pass away, but the man who does the will of God lives for ever.'[1]

[1] 1 John 2:17

taking it further

key themes for study

Divine sovereignty and human responsibility. John Harris describes the relationship between these two truths as 'Scripture's most unfathomable paradox', and raises many thought-provoking questions: 'Can the future be changed? Is history predetermined? Can God's judgement be avoided? Can God's blessings be lost? Does the fulfilment of prophecy depend upon human response?' For the validity of both truths, even though we find it hard to reconcile them, see Acts 2:23. For an application of what this paradox means in practice, consider John Harris's further comment: 'Jeroboam seeks the answer he wants by manipulating others but God intervenes, thwarting his scheme.'

God's patience. 'As the slow demise of the kings of Judah clearly shows, God's patience lasts a long time but eventually he requires a response.' We may compare Paul's teaching that 'God's kindness' is meant to lead us towards repentance.[1]

for reflection/discussion

Do you know any 'authoritarian, ruthless, hard-line' leaders who 'consider complaints and dissatisfaction a threat to their position rather than opportunities for reconciliation, responding instead by abusing their power as if it is a force to be wielded "harshly"' (1 Kings 12:13)? Of course none of us would ever behave like that, would we?

for specific application

'The yoke Jesus offers implies discipline as well as rest. Those who seek this rest must follow the path of service and humility.' What might this mean in practice for you this week?

'Temptation comes from unexpected places and ... we are most vulnerable after exceptional spiritual experiences.' What can you do to win the battle over temptation when you are at your most vulnerable?

[1] Rom 2:4

can faith recover?

G od tests our faith, not because he rejects us, but because he loves us![1] He sometimes puts us on the spot, forcing us either to renew our faith and press on, or give up the play-acting and be 'outed' as closet unbelievers.

Elijah was called by the Lord to stage a national stoppage. The economy was booming, thanks to the worldly-wise policies of Omri, Ahab's father. But Elijah unceremoniously foretells a drought (17:1) – something every Israelite dreaded. The long dry period hit the country's agrarian economy hard. And the government branded Elijah a traitor! Well into the third rainless year, Elijah reappeared to confront national representatives on Mount Carmel in one of the most tense and powerful scenes in the Bible. He demanded they settle their religious loyalty once and for all (18:21).

It's helpful to distinguish three perspectives in the story of Elijah. First, the ninth century BC drama, involving the key actors in the power struggle for the northern kingdom's soul: Elijah, Ahab and Jezebel. Secondly, there are the first readers of the books of Kings – the people of Judah during Babylonian exile in the early sixth century BC. The third horizon comes over 25 centuries later – you and me, our churches and our nations today.

The common factor in all three horizons is a challenge to faith. At Carmel, the people were sitting on the fence: whom would they serve? The Lord? Or Baal? Three centuries later, exiled Judah was struggling to find a way back to faith from the despair which engulfed them following the traumatic loss of country, Temple and king. And for us today, perhaps the key challenge is to discover that the Elijah story is not locally and historically constrained. As we live in this narrative over the next ten days, may we reaffirm our faith, through God's meeting with us, as his master-story intersects with our personal stories!

Fergus Macdonald

1 **Deut 8:16; Heb 12:4–6**

path to empowerment

'Lord, teach me that the secret of spiritual power in public is to be prepared by you in private.'

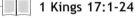

1 Kings 17:1-24

nearly one-third of the two books of Kings focuses on the 34-year period covering the reigns of Ahab and his two sons. Why? First, Ahab attacked the purity of Israel's worship. As if the idolatry of Jeroboam were not enough, he introduced the polytheism of Jezebel, devotee of Baal Melqart of Tyre (16:30–33). Secondly, the powerful resistance of Elijah to this royal policy of paganisation highlights the unique power of the Lord's prophets as movers and shakers for truth in moments of national crisis. The relevance of the Elijah story for the first readers of Kings is obvious; sorely tempted to adopt the religious amalgam of their captors, they were reluctant to heed the words of Jeremiah, Ezekiel and others.[1]

Apart from making his dramatic announcement of drought, Elijah is in hiding, first at Kerith, roughly in his home territory, and then in Zarephath, deep in the 'Baal belt'. The Lord was, of course, protecting him from Ahab. But he was also preparing him for the great public contest on Mount Carmel. As three miracles unfold, we see the prophet moving progressively from passive to active mode. At Kerith he simply waits for the ravens to feed him. On arrival at Zarephath, he announces to the protesting widow what God will do. Later, when the widow's son stops breathing, he becomes proactive and the Lord hears him. The widow's confession (v 24) underlines that Elijah is now ready to go on the offensive and confront Baal in the public arena. As then, so now. The secret of spiritual power in our public persona is to be prepared by the Lord in our private walk with him!

God proves us before he uses us. Bring to him any sense of frustration or disappointment you may be feeling as regards your work in his service.

[1] Jer 44:15–19; Ezek 20:32

an unlikely partnership

'Lord, help me to work more effectively with people I find difficult.'

1 Kings 18:1-19

i n terms of sheer courage and determination, Elijah is often compared to Moses confronting Pharaoh and David defying Goliath. A man of extraordinary spiritual power, he gained the crucial victory for the Lord in a life-and-death struggle with Baalism. But he did not achieve this alone – something he himself at times forgot! Without the cooperation of people like Obadiah, Micaiah and others unnamed, the nation could not have been turned around!

Elijah was a 'loner'. He enters the narrative abruptly and just as suddenly leaves it, only to enter again later on. When moved by the Spirit, he throws caution to the wind (v 12a). Obadiah, on the other hand, was a team player, a man of routine, good order and due process. He was brave, but – understandably – cautious. While Elijah was in favour of facing up to issues, he was a gradualist, believing infiltration – not confrontation – was the way forward. And yet God willed the charismatic prophet and the cautious administrator to work together! Obadiah was terrified at the prospect (vs 9,12,14)! And Elijah showed scant appreciation of the grave risks Obadiah had run in the Lord's cause (v 13). Clearly it was not an easy partnership. But it was effective. Although disparate, the partnership did not become dysfunctional. Why? Because Elijah and Obadiah worked through their differences: the prophet assured the administrator on oath that he would not renege on his purpose (v 15), and the civil servant reconsidered his earlier refusal to risk job and life. In the church today, the key to advancing the kingdom is again a combination of human partnership and divine power. The power is not our responsibility, but the partnership is!

World evangelisation requires 'the whole church to take the whole gospel to the whole world … We pledge ourselves to seek a deeper unity in truth, worship, holiness and mission.'[1]

[1] **Lausanne Covenant, 1974**

national awakening

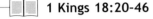

*'O Lᴏʀᴅ, revive your work in the midst of the years! ... In
wrath remember mercy' (NKJV).*[1]

1 Kings 18:20-46

many Western Christians fear that their national cultures are so
secularised that they may never reflect biblical values. They
are tempted to conclude that the church of the future is
destined to exist only as a subculture. The original readers of
1 and 2 Kings were in a similar situation – only worse. Their
religious community had been destroyed and many of its
members forcibly transported to a foreign land where Marduk
and other strange deities were worshiped. Not surprisingly, they
wondered if their community of faith could survive.[2]

As the story of Elijah's victory over Baal encouraged the exiles in
Babylon to recover their faith in the power of the Word of God
to reverse spiritual decline and catastrophe,[3] so also it can
encourage us today to respond to the call of Lesslie Newbigin
(1909–98) and others to affirm the gospel as public truth.

The bottom line is that it was the Lord, not Obadiah or Elijah,
who turned the nation around. 'Elijah is God's servant (vs 15,36)
in this narrative, not a wonder-working hero. He offers prayer
(vs 36,37, 42) rather than the performance of miracles. The
climactic acclamation is not that Elijah is a man of God
(compare 17:24) but that Yahweh is God'.[4] Of course, the choice
of the people was vital. Their silence in verse 21 was, in effect, a
refusal to make a choice. But Elijah skilfully persuades them to
become open to change (v 24). Still today the crucial step is to
convince people to be willing to choose for or against Christ.
We may not all be prophets, but all are witnesses![5]

*'If we really believe in something, we have no choice but to
go further' (Graham Greene, 1904–91).*

1 Hab 3:2 **2 Ezek 37:11** **3 Isa 55:10–13** **4 RD Nelson,** *1 and 2 Kings* **5 Acts 1:8**

'I've had enough, Lord!'

'We promise according to our hopes, and perform according to our fears.'[1] *Thank God that he understands us perfectly.*

1 Kings 19:1-21

elijah's post-Carmel depression may have arisen because he regarded the dramatic triumph over Baalism as the end of the conflict. Caught off-guard by the determined ruthlessness of Jezebel, he panicked and fled. So, having won a decisive battle, he was now in danger of losing the war! Elijah's burnout (a textbook example of depression?) defied rational judgment! He forgets Obadiah's 100 prophets and ignores the national affirmation of faith on Carmel. In Elijah's mind, the people replace Jezebel as the villain of the piece (vs 10,14), and a decisive victory appears as a crushing defeat! His distorted memory produces both exaggerated self-loathing and inflated self-importance.

But Elijah was not allowed to relinquish his prophetic office. The Lord sustained him under the broom tree in the desert, and recommissioned him outside the cave at Horeb. In the symbolism of verses 11 and 12, the Lord appears to tell his prophet that the next phase in his ministry will be different. The emphasis would not be so much on spectacular demonstrations of God's power as on communicating the words he will hear from God. Victory was not to be immediate, and would be achieved by others – most notably Jehu and Elisha – whom Elijah is instructed to anoint (vs 15–17). 'Elijah must be content to being *part* of the plan, and not *the plan itself*' (Iain Provan, *1 and 2 Kings*, NIBC). The promise of a future that would transcend the prophet's success and failure was designed to bring hope first to Elijah, then to the Babylonian exiles, and now to us! Does your church have a sense of being the community of the future?

'It is impossible for that man to despair who remembers that his helper is omnipotent'.[2] *Spend some time in prayer, seeking your Father's will for the next stage of the journey.*

[1] **Duc de la Rochefoucauld, 1613–80** [2] **Jeremy Taylor, 1613–67**

covered with grace

'Lord, you desire truth in my inner parts. Give me courage to respond to the probing of your Spirit.'

Psalm 32

Who wouldn't want joy, new energy and better health? These were aspects of David's experience when he came to terms with God's forgiveness, after wrestling with shame and guilt. The two opening verses give four images of forgiveness. The first is release; the Hebrew for 'forgiven' implies a load has been lifted away. The next is almost the opposite. Sin 'covered' is a frequent Old Testament picture of sacrificial atonement[1] though verse 5 makes clear it is not a cover-up. When sin is covered over with the generous, costly forgiveness of God, it is dissolved and transformed into a layer of experience that is the foundation for a mature spiritual life. We speak of debts being covered and the third phrase here moves into a numerical or financial metaphor; God is not keeping a note of the bill for later repayment. But fourthly, in the person who faces up to and confesses the sin, the tendency for self-deceit is being counteracted and spiritual honesty being acquired.

The apostle Paul noticed the verbal similarity between this reference to God not keeping a sin account for David, and the way God is described as 'crediting' righteousness to Abraham.[2] The connecting factor is their faith. This psalm ends with the apparently sharp distinction between the wicked and the righteous, which we frequently find in the book of Psalms. But the context has underlined that the righteous are not sinless people; they are justified people. Their life of faith begins and develops by trusting God for forgiveness for their falls, as well as staying close enough to God to be guided, not with lists of rules like leading reins (verse 9), but in a relationship with God that fully engages mind and will.

'Let me not grow casual about your forgiveness, O Christ.'
'O make me understand it, help me to take it in, what it meant to you, the Holy One, to bear away my sin.'[3]

[1] Lev 16:15,16 [2] Rom 4:3–7; see Gen 16:6 [3] Katherine Kelly, 1869–1942

good news for a change!

'To him who remains in this world, no repentance is too late.
The approach to God's mercy is open.'[1]

1 Kings 20:1-21

t he account in today's and tomorrow's readings of the Israelite-Syrian war interrupts the story of Elijah, but it's not a digression. Rather, it is a highly significant and integral part of the Elijah-Ahab narrative. This temporary break in the storyline emphasises that Elijah, however effective he had been on Carmel, was not indispensable. The key role played by anonymous prophets in this chapter demonstrates the invalidity of Elijah's melancholy claim to be the only true remaining prophet (19:10,14). For the moment Elijah is relegated to the sidelines, as we observe the bold witness of some of those 7,000 who would not bow to Baal.

Today's reading also demonstrates that, for all his evil, Ahab was not yet considered to be beyond redemption. For a change, he receives good news from a prophet (v 13). God's promise that the Syrian siege of Samaria would fail echoes the exodus: 'Then you will know that I am the LORD'.[2] Clearly, Ahab is being given another opportunity to reaffirm the national covenant with God. The prophet's message of good news reminded the king that, in spite of his own past failures, the renewal of the covenant on Carmel meant that the Lord was the same God, and Israel the same covenant people, as at the exodus. The prophetic intervention was a sign that the Lord in his great mercy was giving Ahab an opportunity to repent – a testimony to God's grace. Would Ahab grasp this undeserved opportunity? Tomorrow we will find out! Meanwhile, let's take to heart two great spiritual realities of God's kingdom. First, no one is indispensable. Secondly, we ought never to write anyone off.

'God often visits us, but most of the time we are not at home.'[3] What do you think God is trying to say to you that you are not eager to hear?

[1] **Cyprian, martyred AD258**   [2] **Compare Exod 6:7**   [3] **French proverb**

the twist in the tale

'The secret of success in life is for a man to be ready for his opportunity when it comes.'[1] What 'success' do we seek?

1 Kings 20:22-43

did Ahab grasp the lifeline thrown to him by a merciful God? Alas! the twist in the tale tells us that he threw away his last opportunity to turn to the living God. The unnamed prophet's parable (vs 37–42) says it all. Ahab was so 'busy here and there' (v 40) ensuring immunity for his royal enemy from prosecution for war crimes (only peasant soldiers die in war!) and negotiating an advantageous trading agreement, that he totally missed the plot. Ahab failed to realise what became clear from verse 13 onwards, that the conflict with Syria was a 'holy war,' analogous to Joshua's conquest of Jericho[2] and Saul's battle with the Amalekites.[3] Ahab violated the 'ban' inherent in such holy wars. So victory, far from leading Ahab to repentance, only sealed his fate as he unwittingly took Ben-Hadad's place under the deadly ban.

Although a holy war ban was impractical in Babylonian captivity, and such things have been revoked by Jesus,[4] Ahab's failure to observe one can be interpreted both as a call to the exiles to re-examine their behaviour in the light of God's Law, and as a challenge to us never to consider our lives exempt from the need for self scrutiny. 'What betrayals and violations of God's will are hidden in the everyday morality of our modern lives? What vital loyalties to God are missed when one is "busy here and there"? What seemingly enlightened actions of mercy (v 31) or shallow "brotherhood" (v 32) may actually turn out to be betrayals of our faith and identity as God's people?' (RD Nelson, *First and Second Kings*, IBC, 1987.) Affirming kingdom values helps us discover our real priorities.

'He who refuses to embrace a unique opportunity loses the prize as surely as if he had failed' (W James, 1842–1910). What opportunity do you need to grasp with both hands?

[1] B Disraeli, 1804–81 [2] Josh 6,7 [3] 1 Sam 15 [4] Matt 5:43–48; 26:52

to covet or to care?

'Abundance consists not so much in material possessions, but in an uncovetous spirit.'[1] 'Lord, please make me generous.'

1 Kings 21:1-29

t he confiscation of Naboth's vineyard graphically illustrates the sin of covetousness – the uninhibited desire for what rightly belongs to another – which Paul tells us first brought him to see his need of salvation.[2] Today covetousness is fanned by consumerist advertising promoting self-indulgent lifestyles. It acts as a spiritual cancer, destroying trust and undermining community. Ahab's capitulation is a grim reminder that the consequences of surrender can be devastating: perjury, murder and theft!

This sordid incident confirms beyond any doubt that Jezebel was, indeed, the ruthless despot earlier references had implied (18:4,13; 19:1,2). She manipulates a legal frame-up involving a trumped up charge of blasphemy which, with the shameful compliance of obsequious local leaders, results in the execution of Naboth and his sons (v 13).[3] Jezebel mocks Ahab's scruples (v 7) because she operates out of a world view based on Baalist nature worship. As in the wild, natural world, where strength seems to prevail over weakness, so in Jezebel's socio-political world view: it was ruthlessly logical for the 'strong' to devour the weak. However, the story of Naboth is about more than the acquisitiveness of Ahab and the arrogance of his queen. The principal actor in the drama is a God who, outraged by the perpetration of injustice and violence, cares so deeply for Naboth and his family that he sends his prophet to foretell judgement on Ahab and Jezebel. Ought not the realisation that the God of Naboth and Elijah is also our God spur us on to ask him to root all covetous desires out of our hearts? And surely it also encourages us to pray that our governments may honour the values Ahab and Jezebel despised: justice, peace and mercy.

'For evil to triumph, it is only necessary for good men to do nothing.'[4] What is God stirring you up to do this week?

1 J Selden, 1584–1654 2 Rom 7:7,8 3 2 Kings 9:26 4 E Burke, 1729–97

truth sought ... and rejected

'If we do not listen to the prophets we shall have to listen to providence.'[1]

📖 **1 Kings 22:1-23**

W riting these notes in the midst of tense public debate about whether America and Britain should go to war against Iraq has helped me to appreciate the momentousness of the decision facing the two kings (vs 3,4), and the accompanying public atmosphere of apprehension. Jehoshaphat – more devout than Ahab (v 43) – suggests seeking divine guidance. Ahab's 400 official prophets were unanimous (v 6). But Jehoshaphat, suspecting flattery, asks to hear a true prophet (v 7). While Micaiah is being sought, the royal prophets continue to prophesy en mass before the enthroned kings (v 10). Maybe the utterance of verse 12 was chanted as a prophetic chorus?

At first, Micaiah sarcastically imitates the official prophets' line (v 15b). But then, after revealing that his inspiration came from a heavenly, not an earthly, throne room (v 19), he delivers a fateful prediction (v 23). Micaiah's assertion that the Lord had put a lying spirit in the mouths of the royal prophets (v 23) underlines the importance of evaluating carefully all claims to speak directly for the Lord.[2] The fact that future verification is the basic biblical test suggests speedy conclusions are unhelpful! The New Testament affirms that God not only overrules the activity of evil powers and people, but even uses them to fulfil his purpose, sometimes by creating delusion in their minds.[3] Perhaps our modern discomfort with such ideas comes from our reluctance to believe what we cannot explain! Micaiah's vision (v 19) anticipates the book of Revelation, and serves as a comforting aide-memoire that unseen heavenly agents are serving us.[4]

'Not everyone who speaks in the spirit is a prophet, but only if he follows the conduct of the Lord' (Teaching of the Twelve Apostles, *first century* AD).[5]

[1] **A Craig, d1985** [2] **Deut 18:21,22** [3] **2 Thess 2:11** [4] **Heb 1:14** [5] **Matt 7:15–23**

sold out to evil!

'That we may be delivered from all tribulation, anger, danger and necessity, let us pray to the Lord'.[1]

1 Kings 22:24-40

J udgement finally catches up with Ahab – the king who perpetrated unparalleled evil, whose death had been predicted by two prophets (20:41,42; 21:19) and towards whom the Lord had exercised extraordinary patience. Ahab seems a pathetic figure. Although not without natural ability (v 39), he was essentially reactive and timid by nature. Throughout much of the biblical narrative he is either dominated by his ambitious pagan wife (19:1,2; 21:5–7), or brow-beaten by Elijah. His weakness was seen most clearly at Carmel (chapter 18). 'Ahab speaks only once in the entire story and having been silenced by Elijah's aggressive and fearless response, he spends the rest of the time doing what the prophet tells him or watching from the sidelines so quietly as to be invisible'.[2]

Paradoxically, in this final and fateful episode – the military campaign to regain Ramoth Gilead – he at last shows initiative. But alas! His new resolve seems to have been motivated by a determination to oppose and, if possible, outwit the Lord. A hardening of heart is evident in his hatred for Micaiah and his determination to prove him wrong (vs 8,26,27). His resort to disguise (v 30) suggests that, for all his bravado, he secretly feared Micaiah's prophecy of doom (v 23), and desperately sought to hide from God as much as from the enemy forces. But all in vain! The 'accidental' nature of his mortal wounding (v 34) reveals that God's sovereignty embraces even apparently random actions. Although Ahab fell in battle, his army retreated safely, fulfilling Micaiah's first vision (v 17) and reassuring exilic readers that, although the Lord had opposed the royal intrigue against Babylon, he had not abandoned his people.

'For a Christian end to our lives, painless, without blame and peaceful, and for a good defence before the fearful judgement of Christ, let us beseech the Lord.'[1]

[1] **From the Liturgy of John Chrysostom** [2] Iain Provan, *1 and 2 Kings*, **NIBC**

contrast and paradox

'Lord, teach me how I can be wholly loyal to you today.'

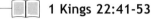

1 Kings 22:41-53

The Elijah cycle is not quite finished, but it's time for a brief update on the southern kingdom. Apart from Ahab's alliance with Jehoshaphat, there has been no mention of Judah in over seven chapters – an indication of the high priority the narrator gives to the confrontation between Elijah and Ahab. Today's reading provides a classic contrast between Jehoshaphat the saint and Ahab the sinner – see the summaries of their respective reigns (vs 43,52). Note both verdicts testify to the power of parental example for good or for ill.

We learn less about Ahaziah (whose story is carried into the next book) than about Jehoshaphat, whose reign is covered in greater detail by Chronicles. Jehoshaphat was a people's king, who initiated extensive educational, legal and religious reforms and built up a strong, well-organised army that secured peace for the nation.[1] But this good man was not without paradoxes! He attempted, but failed, to remove the forbidden high places – local pagan shrines taken over for worship of the Lord (v 43)[2] – and received a prophetic rebuke for making a treaty with Israel, involving military assistance in the abortive Ramoth Gilead campaign[3] and a fateful royal marriage.[4] This marriage led to the gravest crisis in the history of the house of David and a disastrous joint shipping venture (vs 48,49).

Saint Jehoshaphat? Yes, but not without flaws! The favourable verdict of both narrator and Chronicler surely encourages all frustrated aspirants to sainthood!

'Lord, I believe; help thou my unbelief!'[5] Bring to God your aspirations and your failures. Thank him that he accepts you in Christ, warts and all.

[1] 2 Chr 17:10–19 [2] 2 Chr 20:33 [3] 2 Chr 19:2 [4] 2 Chr 18:1 [5] Mark 9:24, AV

taking it further

key themes for study

Greed. Fergus Macdonald defines covetousness as 'the uninhibited desire for what rightly belongs to another.' Ahab's greed as regards Naboth's vineyard results in the most severe judgement. Later prophets continue the theme of God's abhorrence of injustice and oppression of the poor.[1]

Prophecy. Elijah is a man of God (17:18) to whom the word of the Lord comes (18:1) and on whom the Spirit of the Lord rests (18:12). He is marked by uncompromising, fearless proclamation of the messages he receives. Several other prophets are mentioned (20:13,22,28,35; 22:8).

Depression. Elijah constitutes a classic case of burnout, an increasing problem for Christian workers in today's world. Scared stiff by Jezebel's threats, he demonstrates 'exaggerated self-loathing and inflated self-importance.' God first cares for his physical needs, then re-commissions him in a way that shows he still has a role to play, but everything does not depend on him!

for reflection/discussion

'Elijah is now ready to go on the offensive and confront Baal in the public arena.' Do we need to do more to 'affirm the gospel as public truth'? How can we make our voice heard?

'The key to advancing the kingdom is a combination of human partnership and divine power.' Which is the greatest need for your church: to partner more effectively with other Christians or to be more expectant of God's power at work?

for specific application

'God tests our faith, not because he rejects us, but because he loves us!' Bring to God any feelings of hurt or doubt that you have had because of things that have been painful for you. Remembering that 'God proves us before he uses us,' re-affirm your trust in God's wisdom and offer yourself afresh to his service.

[1] Isa 1:15–17; Amos 5:11–15; Mic 6:8

God's authority and love

Sing or play a favourite worship song. What words or theme catch your attention most?

 Psalm 33

The structure of this psalm could provide a good model for someone planning an act of worship. It starts with joyful singing, new songs as well as old accompanied by musical instruments skilfully played. It ends with a declaration of commitment; the worshippers are to depart with their hope and trust in God renewed. In between, the psalm presents a global vision of God with the great themes of Israel's faith laid out.

Creation is described in vivid metaphors indicating how small the universe is beside God. But creation is not the opening theme. The psalmist leads with the moral character of God (vs 4,5), as if to emphasise that God's justice and loving faithfulness are built into the very fabric of the world that came into being, as God spoke. The human race in particular is not developing randomly. Despite rebellion, its history follows God's plan (vs 10,11). At the centre of that is the choice of a people to live in a covenant of faithful love with God (v 12). The psalm lives with the tension between the all-powerful Creator who forms the hearts and deserves the reverent fear of all human beings and the great Lover who jealously keeps his eyes on his own.

The same tension is there for those of us who work with others in companies, institutions or cooperatives. Justice for all in the world and a fair sharing of land and resources should be our goal but the welfare of colleagues for whom we are responsible often seems to hinge on quick, competitive decisions that harm others if they benefit us. There are no easy answers for resolving this dilemma in a complex and sin-ridden world.

Worshipping God together is a good time to remind ourselves that all human authority is a trust from God.[1] We depend on his guidance to use it justly and well.

[1] Rom 13:1; Titus 3:1,2; 1 Pet 2:13–17

Christ's wonderful humility

t here is a huge difference between a snapshot, a careful photograph and a painting. If you were to take a 'snapshot', a quick summary, of the letter to the Philippians, you would probably say that joy is its main theme. Certainly, joy figures memorably. If instead you took a careful 'photograph' of it, you would decide that Christ is central, permeating the whole picture – he is referred to in more than half the verses. The whole letter has the aroma of Christ, so it would seem that he is the dominant theme. However, if you did a 'painting' of the letter, gazing more deeply at its central themes, you might begin to see that it is not just our Lord, but one aspect of his character which is dominant: and that is his amazing humility.

In our approach to Philippians we need to be ready to see and respond to Christ's humility, which was the great need of the church in Philippi. Some of its members were at loggerheads with each other. The defences of human pride needed to be smashed, and the true Spirit of Christ allowed to change individuals and the whole fellowship: humility was to be at the top of their agenda. So right from the start, Paul specifically avoids his normal phrasing of himself as an apostle, with Timothy as his brother. Instead, he puts Timothy on the same level as himself – both simply servants of Christ Jesus. This theme is emphasised again and again, in the magnificent summary of Christ's humble attitude in chapter 2, and the 'everything a loss' passage of chapter 3, which I find deeply moving. Chapter 4's readiness to be content, whether in plenty or need, provides one last example.

Philippi's general atmosphere was the very opposite of this Christlike humility. Militarism dominated the city. Philip II (father of Alexander the Great) had founded it in 358BC, and named it after himself. Then in 31BC, Octavian (later called Augustus) repopulated the city with Roman soldiers, mainly war veterans, especially those honoured in battle. Humility was despised in general in Roman society, but especially so in a population where pride, personal honour, power, authority and aggression were commonplace. It is not surprising that the church that emerged in the city was infected with this virus. The dispute between Euodia and Syntyche in chapter 4 may well reflect leadership rivalries between the growing number of house churches after the city church had its initial beginnings in one woman's house.[1]

This was mostly a Gentile city, so the church was largely made up of Gentile converts.[2] Judaisers, who aimed to make Gentile converts submit to Jewish customs, were now disturbing the church in Philippi with the demand that all should be circumcised. Paul attacks them strongly in chapter 3.

Overall, deep affection permeates the letter. It was at Philippi that Lydia (a Gentile) had opened her house for the church, that Paul had met the possessed slave-girl and had been thrown into prison, until the earthquake and the conversion of the Philippian jailer. What days they were! Paul loved this church, and they clearly loved and supported him (chapter 4). An additional dimension is given to the letter by the imminent possibility of Paul's martyrdom. Here he is in prison (commentaries discuss at length its possible location). He awaits the outcome of his trial, not knowing whether he will live or die. It is not death he is concerned about, however, but glorifying his Lord whatever happens. We have here an incomparable expression of devotion and dedication. A rich (but challenging) feast awaits us as we study it together. Open your heart!

Michael Baughen

[1] Acts 16:12–16 [2] see Rom 15:26,27

all loves excelling

'Love divine … boundless love that makes us whole.'1 'Lord, help me show love, and long for its dominance in the church.'

Philippians 1:1-11

floods of water devastate; floods of love exhilarate. Paul is in the full flood of God's love. The gospel blazes in his heart – those who share it bring him joy (v 5), and his heart aches for the Philippians (vs 7,8). He shows this love in warm encouragement, putting his arm round his loved ones, encouraging them with confidence in their good work (v 6) and their sharing in God's grace (v 7). All of us welcome encouragement. I wish I had given more of it to others in my life. How often do *we* tell others that we 'thank God' for them in our prayers (v 3)? Paul also goes the 'extra mile' that God's love inspires, in saying he prays for and loves them *all* (vs 4,7), however awkward – we need that same grace. To add to the challenge, he reminds us he is 'in chains' (v 7), so he had every excuse to think of himself more than others.

How may our hearts be flooded more with God's love? One of the main ways, ignored by most, is to pray as Paul does here (vs 9–11) – for spiritual rather than physical needs – and to request prayer for ourselves in these terms. Verse 3 indicates that he works in a framework of regular, organised prayer, learnt from his Rabbinic training. Conscious perhaps of the disagreements in Philippi, Paul prays for the full flood of God's love in verse 9 ('abound' can be translated 'overflow'). This is not a vague love but one that discerns right from wrong in actions and attitudes – a love which is deepening constantly in the understanding of what *God's* love involves. Such prayer transforms the church … and that means us!

Does your prayer life need a major overhaul? If so, act: get a booklet, write down the names of all the members of your church, and pray like Paul.

1 **Charles Wesley, 1707–88**

advancing the gospel

Prepare for reading with this focus: 'How beautiful … are the feet of those who bring good news … who proclaim salvation.'[1]

Philippians 1:12-18a

h ere is a stunning example of gospel first and self second. Paul is a 'so that' Christian. He looks for a higher purpose in the circumstances that engulf him.[2] Whereas for most of us the problems of life would fill the picture, for Paul it is the gospel which does so, with his own situation becoming merely the frame.

The gospel is advancing (v 12). The Greek word here for 'advance' was sometimes used for clearing a path through a jungle. When so much of our thought about God today is a messy jungle, there needs to be a path cut for the gospel. So many things block the way, but one way that path can begin is by seeing a Christian tackle suffering – even terminal illness – with grace, courage and a gospel priority. A contact of mine reached certainty about God's existence by a Christian couple's reaction to their child's death. Similarly, the impact on Paul's guards would have first been through his positive attitude to imprisonment. As a result they became open to the gospel message. Another great result of this was in the stimulation to Paul's fellow Christians to become bolder in proclaiming the gospel. Would the gospel's impact have been more if Paul had been free? It is not a question he wishes to address. He deals with where he is; not where he might be.

The next verses (vs 15–18a) leave me winded. To rejoice when the gospel is preached, even from rivalry (like another church opening opposite ours), or to rejoice when nearby churches seem more 'successful' with the gospel, takes more grace than most of us possess. But it is vital if we are to put gospel first and self second.

'Lord Jesus, please strengthen me in witness for you; purge from me any streak of rivalry. Enable me always to rejoice wherever your name is uplifted and your gospel is preached.'

1 Isa 52:7 2 See 2 Cor 1:4; 4:10,11

exalting Christ

'Lord, help me to be ruthlessly honest with myself, in seeking the primary aim of my life.'

Philippians 1:18b-26

paul does not just lay himself on the sacrificial altar here. He is not primarily concerned with how he might die, what suffering he might endure, what physical pain might consume him. He goes much further. He has already received strong support from the Spirit of Christ, and knows it; thus, he knows too how strong the support would be in his coming trial, possibly leading to deliverance.[1] He knows that could benefit the Philippians. But he goes much further. He is blazing with one aim and desire over everything else: to exalt Christ in his body (v 20).

Here is no hesitation or half-heartedness. Like a runner stretching forward, he even 'eagerly expects' that he will not be ashamed or lack courage but actually fulfil his aim whatever happens. He can raise his eyes to the wonderful prospect of being with Christ, knowing it to be far better (v 23). That will inspire him, as it has inspired thousands of martyrs in history. But it is the exaltation of Christ that drives these glorious verses and drives Paul's life. To him 'to live is Christ' (v 21).

Paul expresses a similar thought in 2 Cor 4:11: 'We who are alive are always being given over to death for Jesus' sake, so that his life may be revealed in our mortal body'. Our bodies are the theatre in which Christ's glory is to be displayed. Problems, illnesses, troubles must not be allowed to be what matters most. We need to keep resetting the aim of our lives. Whether and however we live or die, the aim overriding all others must be the exaltation of Christ in our bodies. Can we say that for us to live is Christ?

Can we now honestly pray: 'Ready for all your perfect will, My acts of faith and love repeat, Till death thy endless mercies seal and make the sacrifice complete'.[2]

[1] **Compare Job 13:16** [2] **Charles Wesley, 1707–88**

worthy of the gospel

'Father, as I read these tests of what it means to walk "worthy of the gospel of Christ", help me apply them honestly.'

Philippians 1:27 - 2:4

t he priority we give to the gospel is seen in our response to suffering for it. Witnesses to the gospel should not be frightened either by opponents (v 28) or by 'whatever happens' (v 27). (The word translated 'frightened' is used of horses shying at the unexpected.) The fact that such a boldness evidences to our opponents our salvation and their destruction is an added spur (v 28), and history has so much evidence of this in the courage of Christians. The worthiness of doing so is heightened by the humbling truth that we suffer 'for him' (v 29). What a privilege! The priority of the gospel is again seen in our attitude to divisions in the church. These are not only destructive, but give strength to the world's antagonism to Christ. Clear-cut unity in the gospel task, however, is a sign to opponents. What can we do about this plague in the church? Perhaps we could start by asking those who elevate secondary issues into division: 'If we both died now and faced our Lord, do you think he would be concerned about this?'

Paul then pauses to directly assault divisive attitudes in church life, knowing how these frustrate the gospel. We all sadly know the traits listed in 2:1–4 that can so harm a church and its witness, including self interest, vain conceit, lack of love and absence of humility. Paul here leads us to look at Christ. Do we experience the blessings of being in him, do we know his love, the comfort of his Spirit, his touch of tenderness and compassion? Yes, we reply. Then that is exactly how we should be to others. We are to be like Christ.

Do these tests show arenas for action? Perhaps they inspire you to restore fellowship with someone? Or to persevere with gospel witness? Or to pray that you might be more Christlike?

the pathway to glory

Come with awe. Ask the Spirit to help you probe more deeply
the profound depths of glory, humility and obedience here.

Philippians 2:5-11

in this jewel of a hymn about our Lord, the argument regarding the priority of the gospel and the humility of its servants is given its supreme expression. Numberless theologians have pored exhaustingly over its theological nuances but in doing so have sometimes deflected from its main aim, which is to show the total humility of Christ.

It is a deliberate act of humility – he 'humbled himself' (v 8). It is the supreme cost of humility – leaving heavenly glory, 'making himself nothing' (the Greek word means 'emptied' and is notably the same as in 'vain – empty – conceit' in v 3). He became essentially human, shared our likeness, and as a servant with unswerving obedience went to the cross. In this light, all the self-interest and divisions of the Philippian church become dust. Our attitude is not just to be *like* that of Christ, but *the same* (v 5)!

How far do we retain in ourselves the human desires for honour, recognition, power and glory? The disciples had them in the upper room. Jesus attacked them visibly by taking off his coat, taking the servant role, washing feet and then returning to his place – an almost exact parallel with the verses we consider today. That lesson hit home then, and so it should here. The exaltation of Christ is a consequence of his humble obedience and not some added honour. Similarly for us,[1] God will lift up all who humble themselves under his mighty hand. So we bow, not with a nod of the head when Jesus is named but with the surrender of our whole life, because he is Lord (v 11). And now – as well as eternally – we heartily proclaim: 'Jesus Christ is Lord'.

Humility makes us door-openers (not doormats!) because it
entails, as for Jesus, unreserved submission to the will of
God. We are called to whole-life humility, as he was.

[1] **1 Pet 5:6**

the daily work-out

*Paul tries persistently to rouse the Philippians. So let us pray:
'Lord, make my ears always open, my will always responsive'.*

Philippians 2:12-18

Paul applies his teaching about Christ immediately ('therefore', v 12). He intends the stunning humility of Christ to have a deep impact, inspiring an active response. He prepares the ground for this next thrust by loving encouragement. 'Dear friends' is actually 'beloved' in the Greek. You can feel his embrace. He praises them for continuing to obey even in his absence. Is there stimulus here to write letters or emails of encouragement to young Christians away from home? In the following challenge you can sense the atmosphere of verses 6–11. Christ made … took … (v 7), humbled himself … became obedient (v 8) – all active words describing how he worked out the saving purpose of his life. Similarly, we are to 'work out' our salvation in verse 12. Glory at our Lord's achievement (v 11) is matched by our need to 'shine' (v 15). His outpouring of himself in sacrifice is echoed in the imagery of verse 17.

'Work out' means 'get something completed.' Salvation is by grace alone, through faith[1] – so this is not about salvation through works, but about working out the saving life we have in Christ, and increasingly submitting our will and actions to God's will and purpose. This includes 'holding out the word of life' (v 16). The Philippians do this well. Paul is more concerned about God's purpose for a church to be 'without blemish',[2] to be holy and thus shining in the darkness (v 15).[3] This perspective takes sin's deceptive deflecting seriously (compare the 'fear and trembling' of verse 12), and calls for radical action to stop the arguing and complaining (v 14). They must work at becoming blameless and pure (vs 14,15).

This passage is aimed primarily at the life of the local church, where divisions and self-interests often obscure the gospel. Is our church at fault? Are we personally at fault? If so, act!

[1] Eph 2:8 [2] Eph 5:27 [3] Dan 12:3

safety in stress

What is the trickiest situation you are facing now? Ask God to store it in his strong room while you talk.

Psalm 34

r elief and thankfulness underpin this psalm. David speaks from a place of safety, but he is aware of a landscape of lurking danger: fears, shame, trouble, hunger, want, broken hearts, crushed spirits, even broken bones. No story in the Bible exactly matches the heading, but in a very similar incident David has a nail-biting, narrow escape.[1]

So the psalm invites us to come into a safe campsite guarded by angels and take time to meet with God. Two key themes in that invitation are based on the senses: to look and to taste.

Make eye contact with God (v 5). There is a quality of prayer that is best conveyed in the language of looking and seeing. It lights up the face and overcomes shame. When we look attentively into the face of another person, we may end up seeing something of ourselves through their reaction to us. So in the attempt to see God, we see more clearly who we are: confused, easily distracted, often disappointed but constantly drawn on by the love of God.

The second invitation (v 8) moves from sight to taste, the most specialised of all the senses, with its focus on feeding. It is often a neglected capacity in busy lives. If we linger and savour things, we can learn to distinguish more flavours and discern excellence in food. Peter linked this verse with the experience of newly baptised Christians who had tasted the word of God and were hungry for more.[2] Paul spoke of moving on to solid food, with the Spirit of God helping us discern truth that is compatible with the wisdom which speaks of a crucified saviour.[3]

It may be hard to set aside your anxieties today, but try to enjoy as much as you can of God's presence and linger over God's word.

[1] **1 Sam 21:10–15** [2] **1 Pet 2:2** [3] **1 Cor 3:1,2**

the highest interest

'Lord, what comes first for me – self-interest or your interests?'

Philippians 2:19-30

imothy's selfless interest in the Philippians and the gospel is contrasted to the self-interest of others (vs 4,21). Paul's readers would know of Timothy's timidity,[1] but also they would know his outstanding qualities: his dedication to stay alongside Paul, even in prison; his readiness as a messenger to undertake the exhausting 80-day round trip ('send … receive', v 19), and his putting first the interests of Jesus Christ (v 22). To say to our Lord, 'I am willing to do anything for you,' without brackets or small print, is to put Christ's interests first, as Paul and Timothy did, and as countless men and women have done in going to dangerous places for Christ. It is to have the selfless humility of our Lord.

Epaphroditus (his name means 'charming') had been sent by the Philippian church to bring their gift to Paul (4:18) and to stay and help him. Paul's appreciation of him in verse 25 shows how excellently he fulfilled that task but that, as a result, he nearly died (vs 27,30). The key phrase in verse 30 is 'risking his life'. The Greek literally means 'gambling with one's life'. The title was used of Christians daring to bury the diseased bodies of dead people, thrown out into the streets by non-Christians, or of caring for those sick with the plague … even enemies. I think of a Christian tending fellow prisoners dying of diseases at the river Kwai, or of Archbishop Janani Luwum confronting Idi Amin and being shot dead – all risk-takers for Christ. So are all who witness to the gospel and care for the welfare of others in places antagonistic to Christ. How this challenges self-interested Christian softness!

Can we look honestly at our life at home, church or work, and write down where self-interest is greater than the interests of Christ and of others? And then resolve how to change?

[1] **2 Tim 1:7; 1 Cor 16:10**

profit and loss

Is my greatest ambition to become more like Christ? 'Lord, increase that ambition in me today.'

Philippians 3:1-11

t he words 'I consider' (v 8) imply a life-resolve to regard privileges and rites as rubbish and profitless (v 7). So he condemns those who try to drag Christians back into legalism (vs 4–7).

'I gain' (v 8) contrasts profit with loss. How profit? Think of marriage. We gain a person and all that they are, plus their family. So when we are in Christ, all that is his becomes ours.[1] It is an increasing experience of 'surpassing greatness' while our being 'found' in him (v 9), through faith alone, has the element of constant wonder.

'I want,' in verse 10, penetrates my soul because it is not written by a new believer but by a man of deep theology, with a track record of Christian service second to none and a Christ-centred life. He still aches to know Christ more. Older Christians like me take note: it is easy to rest back on our spiritual knowledge and experience whereas we should still be eagerly longing to enter more deeply into the heart of Christ and to be more fully illuminated by him. As some communion services urge, we are 'to feed on him in our hearts by faith'.

The further along the Christian path we go the more we see our weaknesses and our need for Christ's resurrection power (v 10) to live like him. We also need to get more deeply into sharing his sufferings in the world, 'so that … the life of Jesus may be revealed'.[2] This stimulates passionate prayer. Verse 11 caps it! 'Attain' is not an indication that Paul is unsure of salvation but that he (of all people!) feels his unworthiness. What humility!

To help you meditate on verse 10 you might like to write it where you will often see it – desk, mirror, computer screen – until it is written in your heart.

[1] 1 Cor 3:21–23 [2] 2 Cor 4:10

straight ahead to glory

Today we are encouraged to see ourselves as marathon runners, focused on the finishing tape. Pray for inspiration!

Philippians 3:12 - 4:1

t he passion of vs 10,11 flows unstoppably into verses 12 onwards (no paragraph break in the Greek). Paul's initial theme is 'press on!' (vs 12–16). Those who, influenced by false teaching, believed humanity to be already perfect, have their balloon pricked. Paul knows perfection can only be at our transformation (v 21) and teases them to live perfectly if they are 'mature' (vs 15,16)! For Paul there is never retirement from Christian growth or calling. Indeed, he inspires those of senior age to 'strain forward', not ruminating on past failure or success, but going hard for the goal … Christ himself.

Then, Paul's cry changes to 'stand firm!' (3:17 – 4:1). Christian role models – those with faithful integrity in all spheres of life – have huge influence, whether in history or the present day. When Paul suggests himself as such a role model, he is not proud but practical – in the early church, it was apostolic witness, not the unwritten New Testament, that gave a guide to Christ-centred life. Thorough Christian integrity is needed today, and we feel deeply with Paul about those who slide into total self-interest, becoming 'enemies of the cross'. The press highlights them; the body of Christ groans; their lives are a waste ('destruction' here is the same word as at the Bethany anointing).[1] To strengthen role model living, Paul points to Philippi's total Romanising in law, dress, language and conduct, which was meant to be attractive to outsiders. So should citizens of heaven be distinctive and attractive. Romans did it for their Emperor, whom they called 'Lord and Saviour'. How much more should we live lives worthy of the true Lord and Saviour (v 20), longing to know him, to serve him faithfully, ready for the glorious transformation!

Let us ask ourselves honestly: am I a faithful role model of what it means to be in Christ? Am I truly becoming more Christlike as I grow older?

[1] Matt 26:8

the beautiful life

Beware familiarity with verses 4-9. Digging into this text takes a lifetime. May I suggest prayer, requesting deeper insight today?

Philippians 4:2-9

W e are now brought down to earth. The earlier plea about humility instead of disagreements is focused on two women: Euodia and Syntyche. Paul's heart aches, seeing the ongoing disagreement (rivalry?) of these leaders (women played prominent roles in the establishing of Macedonian churches,[1] reflecting their shared leadership in society generally). Their gospel-ardour, hard work and eternal destiny are not in doubt. The damaging fault is their not 'considering others better than themselves' (2:3). Like Paul, our hearts ache when we see this in our churches; like Paul, we must tackle it.

The picture painted for us in verses 4–9 portrays the 'beautiful life' Christ expects in us, alongside gospel witness and service. While joy in most people is on-off, geared to circumstance, in the believer it is geared to the Lord, and so never changes,[2] even though surface happiness varies. It spawns magnanimity ('gentleness', v 5), which is mercy, generosity, going the extra mile. So 'the Lord is near' may be a reminder of his amazing magnanimity. Our Lord's nearness also encourages us to see prayer as talking to him intimately and openly, rather than specifying how he should answer. It is this, springing from total trust, that brings amazing peace. Peace is reinforced as we are increasingly freed from the falsity and impurity that infects this world. Our lives witness powerfully when built on truth (total integrity) and right, as well as on what is noble (honourable), pure and excellent (v 8). We all long to develop strongly like this, but hear it clearly: this will only happen if we constantly think about these things. Then the wonderful outcome will be living in harmony with 'the God of peace'.

What was illuminated for you? Go on thinking about it today. Take action if it is required. Write out verse 8 and meditate on one aspect each day for a week.

[1] **Acts 16:14,40; 17:4,12** [2] **Hab 3:17–19**

the 'can-can' christian

Paul's rejoicing (4:10) springs not only from his faith but also from his attitude of contentment.

Philippians 4:10-23

a dilemma faces Paul. He needs to say 'thank you' for the Philippians' gifts (vs 15,16,18) but he does not want to compromise the principle he has 'learnt' (the word indicates it has not been easy) of contentment, whatever his state. That principle challenges the want-want, lottery-crazy, win-the-biggest-prizes plague of society today. It is also the key to 'high dividends' from 'religion'.[1] The giver is always more contented than the 'getter'.[2] So Paul's 'thank you' shifts to the attitude behind the gifts – the concern (v 10), the goodness (v 14) which becomes 'credited to their account' (v 17) and reflects Old Testament sacrifices (v 18).[3] It is vital that personal and church giving reflect this spiritual dimension. God is no man's debtor over our needs (v 11), but there is no justification here of a prosperity gospel. The lavishness of God is in his grace, with 'all wisdom and understanding'.[4] Yet Paul's contentment about his state is only one aspect of his over-riding conviction that he can do everything through him who gives him strength (v 13). This had fired his whole apostolic task – speaking, travelling, pioneering, facing dangers, imprisonments … whatever happened. Christian leaders who are discontented with their lot should expose themselves to this passage.

This 'can' is so positive! It leaves no place for the cannots. It grasps the vision, leaps beyond the safety net, advances the kingdom and believes that with God the impossible becomes possible. His final greetings demonstrate that. How many would expect members of Caesar's household to come to faith, and so face persecution for refusing to call Caesar 'Lord'? Impossible? Not with faith, prayer, witness and the 'I can, through him' conviction!

Do we need to repent? Grumbling or kicking against what God is doing with us needs repentance. Let us change our attitude, and seek to burn afresh with 'I can through him'.

[1] **1 Tim 6:6, REB** [2] **Acts 20:35** [3] **Exod 29:18** [4] **Eph 1:8**

taking it further

key themes for study

The humility of Christ. The key passage here (2:5–11) describing Christ, who first 'made himself nothing' (NIV; or 'emptied himself', NRSV) and then 'humbled himself' to death on a cross, is the basis for an appeal that the Philippian church 'in humility consider others better than yourselves' (2:3). Other passages show how much they need this exhortation to 'stand firm in one spirit' (1:27), especially the reference to the rivalry of Euodia and Syntyche (4:2,3).

Affection. Deep mutual affection between Paul and the church 'permeates the letter.' Paul opens his heart and reveals how much the believers meant to him (1:4,7,8), and how much he appreciated their faithful support (1:5; 4:14–18). Their 'fellowship' in the gospel was almost like a business partnership, except that it was based on the love of Christ!

Christ-centred living. 'It is not death he (Paul) is concerned about … but glorifying his Lord whatever happens' (see 1:20–25). The 'incomparable expression of devotion and dedication' in these verses is matched by Paul's later declaration that he has happily given up everything to 'gain Christ and be found in him,' to 'know Christ, both the power of his resurrection and participation in his sufferings' (3:10a, Gordon Fee's translation).

for reflection/discussion

Describing Philippi's Roman ethos, Michael Baughen comments that 'pride, personal honour … and aggression would have been commonplace … it is not surprising that the church … was infected with this virus.' What particular issues do churches in your area face because of the values held by the local community?

for specific application

The letter shows us several interesting characters: Timothy (1:1; 2:19–23); Epaphroditus (2:25–30); the 'loyal yoke-fellow' (4:3). What qualities do you see in each that you could ask God to increase in you?

○ **David Urquhart**

reasons why
the church must change

t he late 20th century house church movement in the UK had a significant influence on my discipleship as a young businessman. Was the Bible teaching, friendship and liveliness a renewal, a revival, or a revolution? For those who joined, and stayed, perhaps it was all of these things, but looking back at it 25 years on – including 18 years as an ordained Anglican minister – the basic church landscape seems virtually unaltered. The number of those attending churches of all Christian denominations in the West remains a very limited proportion of the population – disciples are being made one by one rather than by the dozen – and the prominent symbols of Christendom, not least the church buildings, have long been stripped of any social significance. But the fact is there has never been more need for spiritual guidance. At the beginning of the 21st century, when it comes to spiritual matters, people are more cynical, indifferent and self-reliant than ever. They are also open to alternative therapies or lifestyles and exotic spiritual practices. So what are the biblical sources of inspiration and guidance for being church in a confused, complicated and even antagonistic community?

"What are the biblical sources of inspiration and guidance for being church?"

A familiar insight into the life of the first Christians is found in Acts 2:42: 'They devoted themselves to the apostles' teaching and to the fellowship, to the breaking of bread and to prayer'. While I do not believe we can deny our history by returning to 'primitive Christianity', these principles of relationship are valid interpretations of Jesus' summary of the Law: 'Love the Lord your God with all your heart and with all your soul and with all your mind' and 'Love your neighbour as yourself'.[1] Jesus also prayed: 'May they be brought to complete unity to let the world know that you sent me and have loved them even as you have loved me'.[2] It is vital that we continue to pray for our church leaders as they face the challenges of seeking more practical expressions of the unity for which Christ prayed. For the rest of us, however, I believe that the key issue in 'being church' is to give priority to our daily relationships with one another and with those amongst whom we live who do not acknowledge Jesus as Lord. This fits in with an increasingly familiar pattern of Christian initiation – first belonging, then believing, then behaving – illustrated by the effectiveness of Alpha and other courses for those enquiring into the Christian faith. Such giving and receiving of each other, following the example of Jesus, can release his converting and transforming power. In Western culture with its over-busyness, we need to make space for relationships both inside and outside the church. I am sure *Encounter with God* readers from

"It is vital that we pray for our church leaders as they face the challenges of seeking unity"

non-Western backgrounds would have some insights for us in how to spend more time listening to and sharing with others.

peace and reconciliation

In May 2002 CMS and USPG, with the hospitality of the Anglican Church in Sri Lanka, convened a South Asian Christian youth conference with some 200 delegates from Pakistan, India, Bangladesh, Nepal, Bhutan and Sri Lanka. The theme was 'Called for Peace'. Afterwards it was noted that 'the coming together of youth in this way was unique. It was a profound and moving experience, particularly for Indian and Pakistani youth, who could meet and form real friendships in the context of a looming war between their countries.' The other remarkable fact was that this meeting, in which we recognised our brokenness and experienced healing of relationships, had come about through cooperation between Western mission agencies, the local Sri Lankan church and a great variety of Christian denominations across the vast area of South Asia. There are many more examples of developing ways of being church in which relationships can flourish. These days we hear much about cell church, church plants, youth church, moving from maintenance to mission, the purpose-driven church, the two-winged church and so on. The phrases may not mean much to everyone yet, but the reality is that we have to come to a new understanding of what we do as church in order to relate to 21st century people's needs. In *The Second Reformation*,[3] William Beckham is insistent that the institutional church is grounded as if it was a one-winged bird. The official structure looks impressive, but without the addition of the other wing – small groups for disciple-making and evangelism – it will not fly again. My experience of trying to plant a church at grass-roots level in a British inner city highlighted the challenge of making new relationships, with the intention of honouring Jesus as Lord, but dispensing with the outmoded trappings of the conventional church. When working from a 'traditional' church base, the difficulty is always in trying to get the institutional wing to make a long-term commitment to the other, 'emerging', wing!

> "The reality is that we have to come to a new understanding in order to relate to 21st century people's needs"

the same but different

Fundamentally, the principles of church are always the same: Christ as head; a holy people; worshipping God the Father; making disciples of Jesus Christ; being a prophetic witness in the power of the Holy Spirit; familiar with suffering; ready to oppose evil; a fellowship called to 'save their lives by losing them'. However, rigorous analysis by writers such as Steve Croft in *Transforming Communities*[4] shows that, no matter which model of church we are familiar with, small groups are an essential balance to larger congregations. If their experience has only been as part of a large congregation, individuals usually mature as Christians much more slowly than they would have done as members of small groups characterised by individual care for their members, an emphasis on welcoming newcomers and with Jesus as their inspiration. The test for me, in affirming the diverse ways of being church, is in the quality of our relationships. Jesus said, 'All men will know that you are my disciples if you love one another'.[5] How does your fellowship match up?

[1] Matt 22:37–39; Deut 6:5; Lev 19:18 [2] John 17:23 [3] Touch, 1997 [4] DLT, 2002 [5] John 13:35

בְּרֵאשִׁית בָּרָא אֱלֹהִים אֵת הַשָּׁמַיִם וְ
הָיְתָה תֹהוּ וָבֹהוּ וְחֹשֶׁךְ עַל־פְּנֵי תְהוֹם
עַל־פְּנֵי הַמָּיִם וַיֹּאמֶר אֱלֹהִים

prophet to the north

t he book of Hosea provides us with a rich vein of God's revelation to his people. Gerhard Maier describes prophecy in the broader sense as 'the passing along of God's utterances through persons.' He comments: 'If the word is passed along then it is not actually the word of the prophet; it remains rather, the word of the Lord'. In the narrower sense he defines prophecy as 'the conveying of divine predictions of the future'.[1] While it is true that we do not have any attesting 'miraculous' signs here (compare Moses),[2] nevertheless Hosea's faithfulness of life, accompanied by the unfolding of the judgements that he foretells, is proof enough that this man was a genuine prophet.

About Hosea's life we know relatively little. We can assume the dates of his prophecy (750–723BC), the final tumultuous years of the northern kingdom (frequently referred to by Hosea as 'Ephraim') before it ultimately succumbed in 722, when Samaria fell after a siege of three years. Whether Hosea lost his life, was exiled with his fellow Israelites, or escaped to the southern kingdom of Judah, is uncertain. His references to the cities of Gilgal, Bethel and Samaria confirm to us that he lived and prophesied in the northern kingdom of Israel.

During the first part of Hosea's ministry, the nation of Israel was relatively calm. The reign of Jeroboam II brought a degree of political and economic stability. In a remarkable way, it was not unlike our present day, with a general prosperity yet at the same time an increasing divide between the 'haves' and the 'have nots'. Alongside this there flourished a deepening corruption of the nation's moral fibre, straddling every segment of society from the courts and the rulers to the streets and the market place. The thirst for 'Baalist' worship pervaded work, leisure, and every aspect of social organisation. Foreign policy was not immune; for later during the ministry of Hosea, throughout the region there was a jockeying for power among the smaller nations as they sought to make opportunistic alliances with one or other of the surrounding stronger states. From 745BC, Assyria dominated the arena and effectively subjugated Israel from 733BC. The final humiliating exile inevitably followed.

Hosea's family life (chapters 1–3) was traumatic to say the least, and graphically recorded. There were three children born within the marriage, although we cannot be certain, with the exception of Jezreel (1:3,4), that he was the natural father of them all. His wife Gomer was probably neither a virgin nor other than promiscuous when he married her – was she simply a cult prostitute, a victim of the degrading false religion of the day, or was she a common 'whore'? Whichever, she was nevertheless a sign to the prophet and to the people, a sign through which we too may hear God speak in love and judgement.

The major themes of the prophecy embrace God's longing for a restored relationship with his people, who are guilty of having broken that relationship through their spiritual adultery. So Hosea calls them unashamedly to repentance, to a new direction of life. Hosea's marriage mirrored the general spiritual and moral chaos of the nation. Thus there was poignancy in his words and pain in his life, as he spoke out fearlessly.

In these oracles Hosea paints strong and dark pictures of judgement, yet never as the final word. God's loving pleas, brought to a pinnacle of longing and promise in chapter 11, will finally hold out hope to these as yet rebellious people. Kidner delightfully describes God as 'by turns … cool … tough … but above all tender'.3

further reading
Elizabeth Achtemeir, *Minor Prophets I*, NIBC, Hendrikson/Paternoster, 1996; Derek Kidner, *The Message of Hosea*, BST, IVP 1981.

David Blair

1 *Biblical Hermeneutics*, **Crossway Books, 1994** 2 **Num 16:28–35** 3 *The Message of Hosea*, **p13**

families: fact or friction?

*'Faithful God, speak to us even in unspeakable circumstances.
Bring light from your Word; reality out of shadow.'*

Hosea 1:1 - 2:13

t o marry a prostitute would seem unthinkable. What a distraction from 'real ministry', we might say! In these early verses ('Go, take…'), God places on Hosea's shoulders what seems like the heaviest of burdens. However, God was doing serious business with him: to speak through him to a disobedient and straying people whose spiritual prostitution was self-evident; to speak through the prophet as a visible sign of his living word. Thus that word is teased out in the telling, terrible meanings of his children's names (vs 4,6,8): the judgement of history; the apparent withdrawal of love; the alienation of God's people. These were the consequences of a spiritual prostitution, sadly not always recognised by those caught up in it. Other 'gods' may deceive us, and will *always* spoil our relationship with the God who brooks no sharing.

In chapter 2 the scene shifts to Gomer, the one whose life and appearance (v 2b) speaks a denial of a true and fulfilling marriage: sexual appetite, short-sighted gains, unfulfilled desires, leading only to a dead end (v 6). In his rebuke, Hosea remarkably longs not for retribution but for restoration. Picture faithless Israel – religiously sophisticated, but spiritually bankrupt. How far is the contemporary church mirrored in these verses? Naked, thirsty, unloving,[1] ever seeking but seldom finding,[2] ensnared by contemporary values, but embittered by a failure to acknowledge God as the source of all we have. Yet there are breaks in the clouds. The fine shafts of the sun's rays bring us to discover God in unexpected circumstances. Verses 10 and 11 of chapter 1 transform the bleak picture into one of living relationships, in a harmony of purpose, under the leadership of 'the LORD our righteousness'.[3]

How do we react to this 'seedy' account of unfaithfulness? Do our spiritual arteries harden or our hearts go out to the careless and disobedient? Pray for discernment, compassion.

[1] Rev 2:4; 3:17 [2] 2 Tim 3:7 [3] Jer 23:6

will God defend me?

If you are brooding over specks in your brother's eye, might you be ignoring a plank in your own?[1]

Psalm 35

t he world is full of violence, and right at this moment some believers somewhere will be in danger, with literal enemies attempting to kill them. Most of us experience aggression in more subtle ways, perhaps in the competitive contexts where we work. Children suffer it in the playground at school. The stream of anger running through this psalm probably indicates the energy the psalmist needs to muster to avoid being overwhelmed by depression and defeat.

Notice how he handles his anger and his longing to be justified. First, he trusts it to God, as the apostle Paul recommends.[2] Human retribution is always deeply flawed; only God can see the true justice in a situation. Secondly, his prayer for vindication is carefully aimed. He asks God to block the enemies as they attack (vs 5–8), and to bring them to shame and dismay (vs 4,26). This could be their opportunity for repentance and change.

The psalmist's distress is heightened by the rejection he feels from people he looked on as friends (vs 11–16). When they were in trouble he would pray for them and grieve with them.[3] Now he finds them distancing themselves, believing rumours and treating him as likely to contaminate them.

Some of the greatest anguish for Christians comes from battles and splits within the church itself. This has been so from the beginning. The New Testament indicates there are times when it is necessary to draw boundaries and exclude, but reluctantly, on a great deal of evidence and with tears.[4] Too often, as here, fellowship is withdrawn on the basis of misrepresentation and with glee (vs 11,15). Food for thought?

It can be a great relief to pour out to God our battle stories, but it is good to intersperse them, as the psalmist does, with songs and shouts of praise.

[1] Matt 7:4 [2] Rom 12:19 [3] 1 Cor 12:26,27 [4] Matt 18:15–17

the sun breaks through!

'Lord, I need to know you in the depths as in the heights.'

Hosea 2:14 - 3:5

t he language of this passage is rich in sexual imagery. Sexuality has generally had a bad press in religious history, largely through a misunderstanding of God's creative purposes. But here, as Kidner writes, 'Instead of banning sexual imagery from religion, God rescues and raises it to portray the ardent love and fidelity which are the essence of his covenant'.[1] Hosea, who had never abandoned his erring spouse, looks to that future 'day' of renewal (vs 16,18,21). So these verses – spoken primarily of Gomer but encompassing the whole people of God – are clothed in the beautiful symbolism of intimacy, as God expresses his desire for a deep, lasting and inner relation with his people. Do we reciprocate that in our day?

The picture of 'betrothal' (a more significant commitment in Israelite custom than our modern 'engagement') heralds God's unwavering promise to be for ever on Israel's side, to stamp them with his mark of 'putting wrongs to right', to draw from them the warm response of devotion. As a consequence, negative threats become positive virtues. Likewise, we are 'on track' as Christian disciples when we allow God to wrap us up in his love! It is one thing to talk of love, but another to show it. I recall how, on a mission 50 years ago, a student colleague of mine scrubbed a filthy one-room hovel in an Edinburgh slum – actions that spoke more powerfully to a pathetic family living without hope than my words ever could. So the trembling, contrite adulteress comes back to a new life. It cost Hosea – money, yes, but more costly by far was his redemptive love. There is a powerful picture here of Jesus – the friend of sinners.

'Your word beat upon my heart until I fell in love with you, and now the universe and everything in it tells me to love you' (The Confessions of Augustine in Modern English).[2]

[1] *The Message of Hosea* [2] Tr SE Wirt, Lion, 1978, p124

don't blame me!

Do I stand condemning others, but remote from reality? 'Lord, help me get to grips with your Word in Scripture today.'

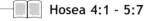

Hosea 4:1 - 5:7

t he broad picture (chapters 1–3) gives way to detailed brushwork (chapters 4–14); the poignancy of Hosea's troubled marriage gives way to a perceptive analysis of the nation's religious shortcomings. Israel's decadence was pervasive (4:2) – evidence that they had rejected Moses' covenant with God.[1]

Also reflect on the picture of a broken environment in 4:3. As I write this, the 2002 Johannesburg Earth Summit begins, and our present concern for the planet is well placed. Yet at the same time we have shut God out, denying him full expression. Instead, we exalt myriad 'spiritualities' – can we see the connection here? Turning from faithful knowledge of God (4:1; 5:4,7a), then as now, inevitably leads in turn to a terrifying abuse of the world we live in. The Israelites were not entirely to blame; their spiritual leaders had sold them short (4:6a,8), bearing the same guilt and sharing in the same spiritual adultery (4:9; 5:1). There were no positive role models. Kidner points out that the task of these leaders was not as guardians of cultic mysteries but as teachers of 'open revelation', 'making wise the simple'[2] – yet they utterly failed to lead people to the heart of God. Patterns of sinful living become a blockage to true repentance (5:4a). Rejection (4:6), judgement (4:9,14; 5:2b) and God's withdrawal from their spurious worship (5:6) follow. This is a bleak scene. The root of the problem is in the Israelites' hearts (5:4b); their corrupt practice is the outcome. Playing fast and loose with alternative 'gods' in any age will always have its payback. Only the Spirit of God residing in our inner beings can ensure that no rival is seated there.

'Christ the King: come to reign in my head as I understand, in my heart as I believe, in my will as I commit myself to act.'

[1] **Exod 20:1–17** [2] *The Message of Hosea,* **quoting Ps 19:7**

blood brothers, or...?

'Some want to live within the sound of church or chapel bell;
I want to run a rescue shop within a yard of hell.'[1]

Hosea 5:8 - 6:11a

h ow do we react to the troubling signs of disorder in our nation's life and the often fragile international alliances our country builds with others to safeguard our so-called freedoms? How far can we interpret God's judgement on human affairs, in all that conspires to threaten our present way of life?

Israel, in dreaded anticipation of international conflict,[2] is called by the prophet to heed these signs (5:8). Israel's king had sought the backing of Assyria (5:13), to shore up his unstable reign, bathed as it was in blood.[3] Israel's 'brotherly' southern neighbours, opportunistic land-grabbers that they were, would not escape God's wrath because of their denial of what God had established in their history (5:10).[4]

Was it a disaster waiting to happen? The very pillars of Israelite society were secretly being dismantled (5:12) in its headlong commitment to what was truly worthless (the synonym of the Hebrew word for 'idols', 5:11). Do not miss God's role pictured in the strongest language (eg 5:14). The only possibility of revival was in repentance. But how deep? As we read 6:1–3, observe the restorative power of God. Recently, I heard Jane, a former prisoner, recounting how she had met Christ. Her sense of God's forgiveness was deep; yet on release she was sucked back into her old ways of prostitution, drugs and petty crime. And God in these instances can seem to be at his wits' end (6:4). With Israel it appears that their 'turning' and their love, in the soulful picture of clearing mists and disappearing dew, was only skin deep. Jane would come back to God again, after the pain of the old ways. How would Israel cope with the pain?

If you can, look again at today's newspaper or watch the TV news. What signs of hope or of despair do you find? Are you ready to pray for revival?

[1] CT Studd, 1862–1931 [2] Jer 4:5; 6:1 [3] 2 Kings 15:16–22 [4] Deut 19:14

a prophet's picture book

Satan does not always attack us head on. He is far more subtle – his goal is, imperceptibly, to deaden our spiritual nerve.

Hosea 6:11b - 7:16

i n this passage, Hosea speaks of a scene that is not so different from ours today. Crime was rampant, in a lawless and morally defenceless society: Hosea exposes corruption at the highest level (7:3,5). While God's intention, as ever, was to bring restoration and healing (6:11b; 7:1) the tragedy was twofold: first, in a failure to grasp the consequences of their evil actions; and second, in an equal failure to sense how the very heart of God was grieved by their deviations, their abject refusal to come back to their spiritual father. The whole picture of moral and spiritual decadence is spelt out in chapter 7, in four powerful images. Take time to allow these to speak:

The fire in the oven (7:4–8). Murderous passions pervade the royal court, stirring intrigue, in an atmosphere of 'half baked-ness' (7:8). 'How better describe a half-fed people, a half-cultured society, a half-lived religion, a half-hearted policy, than a half-baked scone?'[1]

Grey hairs (7:9b–10). A remarkable yet pathetic picture of Israel, totally unaware of its perilous state.[2]

The senseless dove (7:11–12). Picturing the folly of Israel's foreign policy, flitting from alliance to alliance, without hope of security.

The faulty weapon (7:16a). The bow with a string too slack to hit the target, symbolising Israel's wholesale abandonment of God.

What powerful images best sum up our contemporary national and international situation? And what will be our response, as Christians committed to reflecting God's heart for our world? Should we not pray for discernment of the times in which we live?

Pray today for all those in authority, and for the victims of injustice. Your prayer can bring about transformation in both circumstances and in the lives of people you know and love.

[1] GA Smith, *The Book of the Twelve Prophets* [2] Luke 18:11; Rev 3:17

a trumpet call

*'Lord of the streets, open my eyes as the Spirit descends.
Help me to find you walking in unexpected corners.'*

Hosea 8:1 - 9:9

r eligion at its best will ask: 'How do we translate our private experiences into the public world we share and make?'[1] Conversely, religion at its worst, with its bad odour filling the nostrils of even the sceptic, is meaningless repetition, institutionalised into irrelevance, and serving only the narrow purposes of those inside the circle. Despite their protestations (8:2,13), the Israelites' religion is rejected by the God who sees the sham of the externals, the mechanics of a worship that should have been suffused with vibrancy and power. Hosea was not alone in echoing God's judgement on a religion without true sacrifice, the panoply of so-called worship without depth and meaning.[2] Neither has God's word any degree of authenticity for them – they see it as 'a strange thing' (8:12). How easy it is for us to get ensnared by contemporary slogans and phraseology that mirrors cultural relativism rather than eternal truth.

Thus their well-worn practices, shot through with corruption and misplaced priorities, suffice only to meet their temporal needs (9:4b) – the missing factor is the presence of God. Their feet will inevitably stumble into judgement and spiritual blindness (v 7b) as they allow the original vision, of a people set apart for their God, to be distorted into a deathly feast (v 4a) when only living bread could sustain.[3] The prophet's lot, running against the tide of opinion, was no easy one (vs 8,9). Misunderstood and ridiculed, his rejection was acknowledged and honoured in Christ's words,[4] since Christ knew that he stood in the same firing line. We who want to win the world for Christ must never assume that the gospel, with all its demands, will be readily embraced.

God may reveal himself by his actions in human history. But we need to allow the prophetic word to explain the meaning of events. Pray that God will give you true discernment today.

1 Chief Rabbi Jonathan Sacks 2 Eg Isa 1:11 3 John 6:32–35 4 Matt 5:10

planning for change

'Holy Spirit, come to me today in my reading. You know my need. Direct my mind, my emotions, my will.'

📖 **Hosea 9:10 - 10:15**

As God's prophet, Hosea was not afraid to speak out. The painful experience of his marriage led him not into retreat but to fearless witness concerning the adulterous behaviour of the Israelite nation. At this point in the prophecy, we find God and Hosea in dialogue together (9:10–14). The poignancy of God's words to Hosea in verse 10 recalls the roots of his love for his people, alongside the roots of their disobedience at Baal Peor.[1] This picture of blighted promise (9:14) is reflected in Hosea's response, as he solemnly affirms God's judgement. How are our personal dialogues with God shaped? Do we listen to his words of passion and judgement, and with what response? If God is reserving judgement for those who persecute Christian believers in our world today, how will he judge us for our failure to pray for those hungry or in prison?[2]

It is made abundantly clear in chapter 10 that destruction and judgement are the inevitable consequences of Israel's sin. Mention of Gibeah (10:9) was a potent reminder of the depraved conduct which had so often soiled the reputation of God's 'chosen people'.[3] In this whole chapter there is an unmistakable air of a destructive reality that springs from alien values killing the seeds of God-given morality (see 10:4b, with its reference to 'poisonous weeds'). God speaks judgement into their spiritual decadence at Bethel, where the heart of worship should have been (see NIV note to 10:8). Yet the hopeful invitation of 10:12 stands out against the backdrop of the varied pictures of past glory and promise (10:1a), and the present moral chaos (10:4,13). Can we discover instructive parallels for our church life today?

What are the competing values you find around you? How do they threaten the church's mission? How should they shape our prayers? How should we lovingly confront them?

[1] **Num 25:1–3** [2] **Matt 25:31–46** [3] **Judg 19:16–30**

breathtaking view of God

Remembering your favourite landscape or sea view might prepare your mind for this psalm.

Psalm 36

many psalms compare sinful people with good ones. This one compares them with the Lord himself. It opens by saying that sinfulness speaks like an oracle. Its message is either warning the godly person (NIV) or enticing the sinner into further sin (NRSV). What is clear is that flattering oneself and plotting harm to others can start the slide into self-deceit and sin. Better to review one's life reverently before God in bed at the end of the day.

From verse 5 there is a background like a nature film, with glimpses of animal life against panoramic views of mountains, sea and sky. Water bubbles in springs and sunlight moves across the sky, highlighting fresh aspects of the view. The delight he takes in the natural world helps the psalmist express his worship and wonder about God. As we saw in Psalm 33:4,5, God's love has faithfulness at its core (v 5), and God's right way is rooted in justice (v 6). Chicks are cared for safely under parental wings and God keeps safely those who take refuge in him, without discrimination.[1] Abundant food and fresh water are freely available at his feast.[2] God's care for all people is bracketed with his care for all creatures (v 6). We should not dismiss the natural world too quickly as merely a visual aid for spiritual truths. Our material life on earth is a foundation for all levels of life with God now and in the future when all creation will be renewed.[3]

The psalm concludes by reminding us that the best way to resist temptations to get entangled with sin is through prayers that fill our plates from the buffet of God's love and righteousness (vs 8,10).

Feast on God today, gratefully aware that you are part of God's creation, as well as someone who can enjoy it. Be humbly aware that, as a sinner, you can spoil it.

[1] Ruth 2:12; Matt 23:37   [2] John 6:51; 7:38   [3] Rom 8:19,20

'all loves excelling'

'Lord, I am hungry for reality, for your love, for eternity. Feed me now through the Word that satisfies like nothing else.'

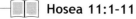

Hosea 11:1-11

The sheer length and depth of God's love is spelt out magnificently in these opening verses. Meditate for a few moments on the verbs of the first four verses and rediscover the mind and heart of God! See, too, the foundational and relational focus of God's dealings with his people – Israel is described as his 'son'. Of course this is more than hinted at throughout the prophecy, but here it reaches its high-water mark, with both historic and prophetic implications – Jesus, the Son of God, is called from Egypt to fulfil his Father's will in bringing salvation,[1] a salvation that has been already gloriously framed in the miracle of the exodus.[2] God's purpose in all this is to nurture, to discipline, that his people might share his holiness, not recoil from it.

Yet was God's not an unrequited love? Hell-bent on their own schemes, Israel refused to turn around, but continued to practise a false and heartless religion and thus threatened to reverse the very direction of audacious grace (v 5). Amazingly, in this context of offer and refusal, God's grace persists. How can we explain it? 'I am God, and not man' (v 9b) is surely the keynote. For God can see beyond their turbulent ways, and down the long hard road to recovery, repentance and renewal; a struggling, winding path on which the prodigal would walk back to true freedom and dignity.[3] So God refuses to hand over his people to everlasting destruction – theirs would be no Admah nor Zeboiim.[4] The senseless dove of chapter 7 will return from insecure environments (v 11) to find its home. In Christ, we are brought home, fearful and thankful. Dare we shrink from such a calling?

'There is a net of love by which you can catch souls.'[5] How are we preparing to build a relational rather than merely a structural 'net' to follow up those who find God's salvation?

1 Matt 2:14,15 2 Exod 12:31 3 Luke 15:17–21 4 Deut 29:23 5 Mother Teresa

the lessons of history

'Take from me, gentle Spirit of God, confusion, tiredness, distraction, and help me focus on your renewing strength.'

Hosea 11:12 - 12:14

G od presents Israel with three serious charges – sin with three faces. And because Hosea is well schooled in historical precedents, he presents God's case against his people with a cutting thrust, linking together past lessons, present realities and future options. That's clear prophetic ministry, and we do well to emulate it. Reflect on the 'pathology' of sin that beset the nation:

Deceit (v 3). It had been Jacob's weakness; yet he, in the process of character transformation, struggled with and found God.[1] Would Israel now, caught in a web of lies, return to rest in God, and live out its historic name?

Fraudulent commercial practice (vs 7,8). Trading in the manner of the surrounding cultures had brought riches, but also self-deception. Israel would become a band of humbled, exiled pilgrims, reminiscent of those delivered out of Egypt[2] – but would they now trust God as their forefathers did (v 9)?

False worship (v 11). Ultimately this is what prompts the prophet's passion. Hosea was not a lone voice, but in a historic line of prophets who 'were sent to make men *think*' (Kidner).[3] Perhaps more significantly, they were called not just for human liberation, but to bring God's people into the experience of redemption and holiness of life. Jacob, in marked contrast, had fled into ignominy and servitude.

The outcome of this lethal combination spells doom for a nation to whom God had revealed his word and his promises. Contemptuous Israel could not expect to live on past reputation. Neither today can our church or nation afford to make such assumptions.

'Surely the LORD is in this place and I was not aware of it'.[4]
Pray that both our communities of faith and our secular leaders will regain that sense of recognition.

1 Gen 32:24–30 2 Num 32:13 3 *The Message of Hosea*, p112 4 Gen 28:16

last chance saloon

'Turn us again, Lord, to face the world, but not without hope, not helpless when confronted with cries of despair.'

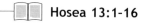

Hosea 13:1-16

this chapter is set in the last years of Hosea's ministry. Hope was in short supply. The northern kingdom was soon to disintegrate in the final conquest by Sargon II of Assyria. Hosea is never simplistic about his nation's history, nor about their prospects. He recognises that their story is a strange mix: the heights of spiritual integrity and the depths of human vacillation. And so he traces in words and pictures the journeyings of a people of great strength and authority, ultimately spoiled and made moribund (v 1b) by their abandonment of God for lesser gods. They were sophisticated idolaters ('cleverly fashioned images … the work of craftsmen', verse 2), but they would vanish in a puff of smoke! The lesser gods of our age will always short-change those who trust them.

As we saw earlier – and it is tragically true throughout their history – Israel's leaders had signally failed them, although they only had themselves to blame (vs 10,11)! Often, even in the most sophisticated democracies, we get the leaders we deserve. Contrast many of the corrupt and weak rulers of this troubled kingdom[1] with the picture we have in verses 4–6a, of a God who delivers, protects and transforms. How do present day leaders, in church and state, measure up to these qualities? Are they too locked into hierarchies and spin, too obsessed by personal power and ambition, to be truly great? Nevertheless, in Israel's darkest moments, and even when facing the most terrible of judgements (vs 15,16), hope was not lost irrevocably. For the promise of death conquered (v 14), looking back to an earlier assurance,[2] points forward to a victory that is realised in Christ.[3]

'The third millennium may bring us back to a situation reminiscent of the early church, where our mission will necessarily be from weakness, foolishness or poverty.'[4]

[1] 1 Kings 14:9 [2] Ps 16:10 [3] 1 Cor 15:55–57 [4] Charles Van Engen

coming home

'Come let us to the Lord our God, with contrite hearts return.'[1] Pause to thank God for his grace and mercy.

Hosea 14:1-9

Our present generation conveys confusing moral signals, reflected in the screaming banner headlines of tabloid journalism. By contrast, here we find both clarity and gentleness: these final, moving verses are a whispering, 'fruit-of-the-Spirit' love call, expressed first by Hosea and then by God himself.

In the symbolism of this chapter there are rich images of the *shalom* of God. From the very beginning of this honest but painful account, Hosea has sought faithfully to reflect God's longing for that intimate, healing relationship with his people. We have observed God speaking to them through Hosea as father to children, husband to wife, lover to beloved. Now, he gently reminds them that these are the necessary prerequisites of true and deep repentance, that will bring them to the bosom of their Father: spontaneity (v 2) and not formalism; humility and not arrogance (v 3); thoughtfulness (v 9a) and not mindless, uncontrolled passions. Hosea does not attempt, in this final scene, to hide the peoples' sins, or the consequences of them. But in feeding their minds and hearts with a pattern of words (v 2) that they might use in turning again to God, he opens the way for God to reveal what he wants to do in them. Read again verses 4–7; witness God's promise to restore his people, a restoration that will bring beauty, strength and fruitfulness.[2] In verse 8, we find both the love and anguish of God expressed – an apt summary of Hosea's message. Sometimes we walk; at other times we stumble. God sees our human fickleness and may sigh with longing. Take time today to allow God to infuse your life with his, being confident of his evergreen constancy and the fruit of his richness.

'We can allow ourselves to be found by God and healed by his love through the concrete and daily practice of trust and gratitude.'[3] Give God space today to rekindle that practice.

[1] J Morrison, 1781 **[2]** John 15:5 **[3]** H Nouwen, *The Return of the Prodigal Son*

taking it further

key themes for study

Spiritual adultery. With imagery based on Hosea's own life experience, we are made to understand the pain which Israel's unfaithfulness brings to God. He longs for them to demonstrate faithfulness and mercy in their interrelationships, seeking the 'knowledge of God' (4:1b, 6:6, NRSV). But, he complains, 'my people are determined to turn from me' (11:7).

Call to repentance. The whole book bears witness to God's longing for a restored relationship with his people; but restoration can only take place if they turn back to him in sincerity, 'trembling' (3:5).

God's love. We learn much in Hosea of the passionate, determined love of God. It seems that there are no lengths the divine Lover will not go to in order to win back his bride, despite her persistent adultery. First he deprives her of his blessings, then he entices her with words of love (2:14), and gives her hope again. The emotion in his cry, 'How can I give you up?' (11:8) is profoundly moving. In the end God is determined to 'heal their waywardness and love them freely' (14:4).

for reflection/discussion

Israel was enjoying political and economic stability. 'It was not unlike our present day, with a general prosperity yet at the same time an increasing divide between the "haves" and the "have nots".' What particular temptations does such prosperity bring?

for specific application

David Blair speaks of our 'terrifying abuse of the world.' What practically can you do this week to care for God's creation?

Faithless Israel was 'religiously sophisticated, but spiritually bankrupt.' Is it time for you to spend some quality time with the Lord, perhaps on retreat?

בְּרֵאשִׁית בָּרָא אֱלֹהִים אֵת הַשָּׁמַיִם וְאֵת
הָיְתָה תֹהוּ וָבֹהוּ וְחֹשֶׁךְ עַל־פְּנֵי תְהוֹם וְרֻ
עַל־פְּנֵי הַמָּיִם: וַיֹּאמֶר

history matters

We're familiar with Henry Ford's pithy dismissal of history as 'more or less bunk'. Less well known is what he went on to say: 'We don't want tradition. We want to live in the present, and the only history that is worth a tinker's damn is the history we make today'.

The Christian Scriptures include a lot of history. But something of Henry Ford's mindset seems to stop us engaging seriously with the historical books of the Bible, other than in a piecemeal way. However, while the church may not give much attention today to its historical Scriptures, the secular world is fascinated by the past. Perhaps this interest relates to living at the start of a new millennium, or to rapid change that makes people want to explore their identity. The historian Simon Schama, whose television series on British history drew three million viewers, quotes Cicero: 'Cultures that wilfully anaesthetise themselves to the past will infantilise themselves. To have no sense … of the pleasures and pains of actually understanding your antiquity is to be robbed of any freedom to shape your posterity'.

The book of 2 Kings opens around the year 853BC with events from the brief reign of Ahab's son Ahaziah in Samaria, capital of the northern kingdom. Meanwhile in Judah, Jehoshaphat is king in Jerusalem.[1] The prophecies of Hosea we've just read coincide with 2 Kings 14–17, narrating events in Israel leading to the Assyrian takeover in 722BC.

The account that reaches us in 1 and 2 Kings is selective; it doesn't attempt balance. The important reign of Omri in the northern kingdom is summarised in six verses[2] while almost a third of 1 and 2 Kings relates the spiritual fireworks of Elijah's and Elisha's times! This is unashamedly theological history.

While a significant body of North American scholarship would date these narratives, or a first edition of them, to Josiah's reign, prior to the exile, most European scholars read 1 and 2 Kings as the final section of a coherent history of God's people written during the exile. Starting with the book of Joshua, it evaluates events – especially the actions of the nation's rulers – in the light of the Deuteronomy account of God's vision for a deeply attractive community of faithful and good people among the surrounding nations.3 Israel's wholesale erosion and distortion of God's vision culminates in the exile. The book of 2 Kings ends with the capture of Samaria by the Assyrians in 722BC and the fall of Jerusalem to the Babylonians in 587BC.

This history sets out to wake anaesthetised people to the activity of God in their past. But it's no exercise in nostalgia; it details starkly why the kingdom failed and the people were exiled despite God's covenant promises. It urgently engages people's imagination with what changes they must make if they are to look forward to a different future. Although scholars hold differing views, it seems likely that the many calls to repent signal a conviction that God would restore and bless Israel again.

There are three levels of meaning to which we need to be alert as we read this history. There is the intimate, domestic level of individual stories, then the level of Jewish political history eight centuries or so before Christ, and finally the level of Scripture's metahistory – the canon of literature that unfolds God's unshakeable purposes from Genesis to Revelation. God speaks to us at all three levels.

Some sober commentators today believe that the Christian church in the West – often as complacent and market-driven as ancient Israel – may soon face catastrophe on the scale of the exile. These ancient history books ask us too, 'How shall we then live?'4 Henry Ford was partly right: the history we make today is history that matters.

further reading
Iain W Provan, *1 and 2 Kings*, NIBC; Carlisle: Paternoster Press, 1995; Brevard S Childs, *Introduction to the Old Testament as Scripture*, London: SCM, 1979.

Pauline Hoggarth

[1] 1 Kings 22:51 [2] 1 Kings 16:23–28 [3] Deut 4:5–8 [4] see Ezek 33:10

power bases

'Lord, in a world of many competing voices, help us to hear you and meet you today in your Word.'

2 Kings 1:1-18

t he Elijah saga of 1 Kings paints a riveting portrait of a prophet and pastor. Courageously and at great personal cost, Elijah has indicted the corrupt political and religious establishment of Ahab, Jezebel and the Baal priests and unswervingly asserted God's sole rule in Israel. In all the drama of this high-profile ministry, he has never lost sight of the needs of the 'little' people – the hungry widow, the sick child, the exploited farmer.[1] As Elijah's life draws to a close, we find him responding unquestioningly to God (vs 3,4), daring to engage with the power bases of the nation – the courtiers (v 3), the armed forces (three times, vs 9,11,13) the king himself (v 15). Proclaiming God's word of judgement is painful. The narrative hints at Elijah's struggle not to run away again from frightening confrontation (v 15, compare 1 Kings 19:2,3). I find myself remembering a modest Aymara pastor in Bolivia who, during the bloody 1980 military coup, distributed Bibles at the gate of the La Paz barracks. In each he had written 'The LORD says, "You shall not kill"'. His brother found him days later in the morgue, tortured and shot.

The issues at the heart of this incident were surely seared on the minds of those who first listened to this brilliantly told story. 'Is it because there is no God in Israel that you are going off to consult Baal-Zebub? … You will certainly die' (vs 3,4,6,16). Three times, three different voices articulate God's requirement of fidelity, and his judgement on those who play fast and loose with him, seeking alternative sources of power that are visible, tangible, seductively controllable.[2]

As we watch and pray about world events, to what extent do narratives like this shape our understanding of power? How might today's passage address this week's news?

1 Deut 24:17–22 **2 Deut 4:15–31; 2 Cor 6:14–18**

telling truth

'The Spirit never abandons the Word as it enters the history of the world. Rather the Spirit makes it a Word for life'.[1]

2 Kings 2:1-25

One reason why the Western church largely bypasses the historical books may be that their juxtaposition of material makes us uneasy. It tests our categories of what constitutes truth. Linear, rational 'history', OK. Narrative that wakes echoes of folk tales, not OK. Throughout 1 and 2 Kings we move between these two types of material. There are the histories of two kingdoms – successions, battles and alliances – that the commentator Brueggemann calls 'the royal tradition of certitude'. These texts shift without warning into an altogether different gear of startling unpredictability, focusing on the activities of God's prophets Micaiah, Elijah and Elisha. Though not poetry, they present us with a perspective on events that is so radically different from the 'official' histories that altered language, rhythms and thought patterns must communicate it. In the last chapter we witnessed the irruption into King Ahaziah's God-dismissing plans of the Lord's decisively different ideas (1:2,16). We heard that triple chorus of inexorable truth. Once again a triple chorus articulates the central issue of this event (vs 2b,4b,6b): in the midst of political chaos and faith under fire, the Lord most certainly lives. The narrative builds to its climax in verse 14 as Elisha boldly tests his faith in the reality and continued activity of the living God.

What are the distinguishing marks of the authentic prophet?[2] Vulnerability seems to be one of them. Elijah's mantle is not Superman's cape! Elisha is plunged immediately into the emotional pressures of misunderstanding (vs 16–18), mockery (vs 23–25) and urgent human need (vs 19–22). The 'packaging' of God's prophetic word is rarely attractive (v 23).

Pray over personal and national need for prophetic wisdom in the light of Ecclesiastes 9:13–18.

[1] Bianchi, *Praying the Word* [2] Deut 18:14–22; Matt 7:15–20; 1 Cor 13:2

stop fretting!

Stop setting the sails of your life for a minute. Let your boat face straight into God's wind and rest.

Psalm 37

J esus could be angry when he encountered evil but he was not fretful about its existence. Quoting this psalm (v 11), he taught that the meek will inherit the earth.[1] He embodied meekness by living joyfully (v 4) and generously (v 21). As a result, he neutralised the power of arrogant, oppressive people when they tried to dominate him (v 17).[2]

In Hebrew, Psalm 37 has 22 stanzas, usually two English verses long. Each begins with a different letter of the Hebrew alphabet, taken in order for easy memorising. It is a good example of the wisdom style of teaching found mainly in the book of Proverbs. It circles round the basic wisdom world view: God's world is well ordered. If we live in relationship with God, behaving as God wants, we will discover that this is the way to flourish and enjoy a good relationship with the earth.

This teacher knows that his pupils will often find this godly wisdom severely challenged by events. In verses 1–11 he stresses the need for secure spiritual roots of trust in God, avoiding loosening them by fretting too much when evil seems successful. In verses 12–26 he develops the contrast between the wicked, who plot (v 12), borrow (v 21) and attack (v 32), and the community of God's faithful people who care for each other and share in times of need. Producing some counter examples to verse 25 misses the point that this is broad-brush painting, teaching for the nursery class. The later verses emphasise a long-term view. Ultimately the wicked will be cut off and destroyed, while the righteous will remain for ever.

'O God, give us grace to accept with serenity the things we cannot change, courage to change the things that should be changed, and the wisdom to know the difference.'

1 Matt 5:5   2 Zech 9:9

man proposes...

'"For my thoughts are not your thoughts, neither are your ways my ways" declares the LORD.'[1]

2 Kings 3:1-27

Oil, rather than wool, may be the commodity at stake (v 4), but in other respects, aspects of this episode echo in the media as I write in late 2002. For advocates of war as a moral crusade, this complex chapter makes sober reading. Moab was one of several pagan nations subservient to Israel since David's reign.[2] Since Ahab's death, Mesha of Moab had aimed to free himself of expensive obligations to Samaria (1:1). Faced by the insurgents, Joram casts around for allies (vs 7,9). Like many political and even religious leaders today, Joram, Ahab's second son, was a cautious syncretist – not a blatant pagan like Jezebel, but a practitioner of the convenient, alternative religion promoted by Jeroboam, first king of Israel (1 Kings 12:26–28). His main ally, Jehoshaphat of Judah, has been in similar circumstances (1 Kings 22:4) when his immediate response was to 'seek the counsel of the LORD'. Now he unquestioningly joins Joram. Only when things go wrong – ironically Joram seems more sensitive to God (vs 10,13b) – does Jehoshaphat consider listening to the Lord (v 11). Imagine listeners' responses as they take in Elisha's initial sarcastic reply (v 13a), his upbeat prophecy, its seeming fulfilment, and the shocking closure (vs 26,27). Mesha's terrible public sacrifice of his son fires the desperate Moabites to a last stand at Kir Hareseth, their capital. God's people turn tail in a crucial reversal. We begin to see the fulfilment of the Deuteronomy warnings.[3] We can't begin to imagine the Lord's feelings as he witnessed Mesha's son die and his people's retreat.[4] The unbreakable connection forged throughout these historical books between people's faithfulness to God and their destiny is powerfully reinforced here.

How does it affect our praying that 'prophets do not control the prophetic word ... God ... can behave in ways that defy our expectations' (I Provan, 1 and 2 Kings)?

[1] Isa 55:8 [2] 2 Sam 8:2 [3] Deut 4:25,26 [4] Deut 18:10; 32:26

rumours of grace

'However simple they may seem, these are the very words, works, judgements, and deeds of … the most high God.'[1]

2 Kings 4:1-17

n o woman ever felt diminished by an encounter with Jesus. Whenever he spent time with women he reversed the patterns of domination and manipulative dependence that wrecked relationships after the fall.[2] There are encouraging rumours of this reversal in the Old Testament too. In times of political and economic turbulence, Boaz related to the alien Ruth in transformed ways.[3] And here the historian paints a vivid portrait, against a background of similarly chaotic times, of Elisha's encounters with several women in different circumstances. In spite of the influence he has with the nation's leaders (3:12), Elisha, like Elijah, remains closely in touch with 'ordinary' people. This chapter reveals a sensitive, compassionate man, who appreciates the generosity of others, a leader who lives an open life among his followers. How does this square with our impressions of contemporary prophetic ministry? Notice how Elisha refuses to take over in the crisis situation that his colleague's widow shares with him. He consults her (v 2) and leaves her unsupervised to act in faith (v 5). The reverberations of Deuteronomy are loud here. Through Moses, God urged generosity, special care for vulnerable widows and orphans, refusal to profit from others' debts. If these neighbours had truly been living as God's people, they wouldn't have lent spare jars (v 3); they would have paid the debts! Jesus deliberately put himself under obligation to the Samaritan woman in asking her for water. Elisha enjoys the imaginative hospitality of a woman in very different social circumstances from the prophet's widow (v 8). She shares his values; notice how unattractive she finds Elisha's offer to put her in touch with her society's power brokers (v 13).

'As God's chosen people … clothe yourselves with compassion, kindness, humility, gentleness and patience.'[4]

[1] Luther, *Preface to the OT*, 1545 **[2]** Gen 3:16; Luke 8:43 **[3]** Ruth 2 **[4]** Col 3:12

feelings and details

'Think of … that divine wisdom which God here lays before you in such simple guise as to quench all pride' (Luther).[1]

2 Kings 4:18-37

recently I helped with some training in Kenya of the writers of Bible guides in a range of vernacular languages. We focused on creative writing and on how we interpret and appropriate Scripture as a word by which to live. I commented that many people now accept that entering into the emotions hinted at in a Bible passage can be a valuable tool for interpretation. People responded with some scepticism! Next morning one of the workshop members bounded in to the first session: 'It works! I've been reading Genesis 22 and imagining the feelings of Isaac walking up that mountain – and his father, carrying the knife. It's made me understand Abraham's faith in quite a new way!'

In a memorable essay on Bible narrative, Eugene Peterson identifies five elements we need to recognise if we are to understand and value the essentially narrative character of Scripture. Every story, he says, has a beginning and an end; in every story catastrophe occurs, rescue is planned, characters develop and every detail has significance.[2] You might like to re-read verses 8–37 and identify these five features. They relate just as clearly to the entire body of history in Joshua to 2 Kings and to the canon of Scripture from Genesis to Revelation. Consider Gehazi's role, try to enter into Elisha's emotions (vs 27,28,35), explore the relationship of wife and husband, reflect on the nature of God expressed here. Hear the echoes of Elijah's ministry (1 Kings 17:17) and the rumours of resurrections still to come.[3] For some of us this may be in some degree our story. The words of verse 28 may come close to expressing our anger and grief at hopes raised and then dashed. Not for a moment does Elisha condemn.

'It's all right … Everything is all right' (vs 23,26). What is needed for our churches to be places where people can be as honest as this woman finally is (v 28)?

[1] *Preface to the Old Testament* [2] *Working the angles* [3] Mark 5:21; Luke 7:11

more rumours of grace

'Our reading is our means of listening to God. "Hear, O Israel!" – this is God's constant call.'[1]

2 Kings 4:38-44

ideally we should not be reading this chapter over three days! This section of narrative is carefully constructed to start and end with a keynote theme of these histories: at the heart of God's nature are generosity and grace, freely available to un-self-sufficient people who place their trust in him. Grace and generosity are also to be hallmarks of his people. Only the number of available jars limited the oil supply (v 6); there was enough to pay debts and allow three people to go on living. In a famine situation a generous man's 20 loaves fed 100 people, with leftovers (v 44). For its original audience this chapter would again have wakened powerful echoes. Surely the author quite deliberately chose stories that prompted memories of the way of life set out for God's people in Moses' extraordinary last sermon, recorded in Deuteronomy. What kind of society did God imagine for his people? One that refused to exploit debts, was ungrudgingly generous to the poor, took thoughtful initiatives to ease others' burdens, responded to the needs of vulnerable people.[2] These are some of the hallmarks of God's vision for his people echoed here in Elisha's encounters. But these stories didn't only stir echoes for the exiles of the hope of God's continuing grace and generosity and life-bringing power. These accounts also reinforce rumours of God's preferred ways of working, rumours which will be confirmed when Jesus comes to respond to the needs of vulnerable people, give back life to the dead and feed the hungry.[3] They will be confirmed again as we encounter the first Christian communities and the lifestyle that attracted thousands to them.[4] They invite us to examine our own measure of faith, of care for others, of dependence on God.

Verse 43 shows us two possible responses when need evidently outstrips provision. Which is normally ours? Are we open to seeing things differently?

1 Bianchi, *Praying the Word* **2 Deut 10:18; 15:7 3 Luke 7:11–15 4 Acts 4:32**

not for profit

'Lord, let us not serve thee with the spirit of bondage ... but with cheerfulness and gladness of children.'[1]

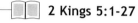

2 Kings 5:1-27

Scarcely a billboard in the city of Lagos does not advertise some pseudo-prophet promising prosperity, healing or success, and guaranteeing blessing in proportion to donations. These perversions of the gospel mostly don't originate in Africa or Latin America. They are lucrative exports from sectors of the Western church of which we should be ashamed. They should also provoke us to think deeply about what it means to offer authentic hope to the poor of our world. John Grisham's powerful novel *The Street Lawyer* has some suggestions!

Among the marks of the authentic prophet – still as relevant today as seven centuries before Christ – is a refusal to exploit financially his or her calling (v 16). Walter Brueggemann, writing of Elijah's ministry, says, 'For all of us in our affluent society who yearn for the freedom and authority to be prophetic, we will find different modes of living only insofar as we disengage, intellectually and economically ... from royal definitions of reality ... Such pastoral-prophetic work requires being fed by ravens, not at the king's table'.[2] Elisha's existence was often as precarious as his mentor's (4:38,42). But he remained unseduced by Naaman's gifts. God rejoices in generosity. He hates greed and lies. Today he sees as penetratingly into our hearts – to our coveting and concealment and self-delusion – as he did into Gehazi's. This is a sober story, reminding us of earlier judgement at Jericho and later judgement in Jerusalem.[3] In stark contrast to Gehazi's greed is the selfless sharing of life-bringing information by an anonymous slave girl. Pray today for Christian migrant workers from places like the Philippines who work in the Gulf States and share their faith with their employers.

'God chose ... the lowly things of this world and the despised things ... so that no one may boast before him'.[4] How do you really feel about this truth?

1 Benjamin Jenks 2 *A Social Reading of the OT* **3 Josh 7:19; Acts 5 4 1 Cor 1:27**

not by might ...

'Almighty God, grant that we who seek the shelter of thy protection ... may serve thee in quietness of spirit.'[1]

2 Kings 6:1-23

d oes God still reverse the laws of nature as this first brief story implies? I remember the director of the Bible Society in Bolivia telling me in Elisha's matter-of-fact tones (vs 6,7) how he and some volunteers went by boat to distribute Bibles to isolated island communities on Lake Titicaca. On the way back, a Galilee-like storm blew up and they began to sink. 'We prayed to the Lord and gradually began to see a circle of completely calm water round the boat. Beyond it, the wind and waves raged on but we got safely to shore!' In a context of service (v 1) and of need (v 5) the Creator God can choose – even today – to reverse nature's laws and work through people who trust him.

An abrupt transition takes us from the intimate and domestic to the larger political arena. The next two chapters focus almost entirely on Israel/Aramean affairs and lead to the violent events that see the end of Ahab's dynasty. It's clear earlier in this history that Elisha is to play some key role in the relationship between Israel and the Arameans.[2] His first contact with them had been the interesting encounter with their military commander (5:1,9,10). Was Naaman perhaps the officer who told the king who was behind his intelligence disaster (v 12)?

Trust in God and alertness to a reality beyond the immediate enabled my Bolivian friends to experience God's power. These qualities characterised Elisha and enabled him to undermine the Aramean king's decisive plans (v 10), to see beyond the enemy lines (vs 16,17) and share reassurance with his frightened servant.

Our sense of powerlessness (v 15) can change as God shifts our perspective (v 16). Turn Elisha's prayer for his servant (v 17) into prayer for yourself.

[1] **Roman Breviary**   [2] **1 Kings 19:13b–17**

God is listening

Approach God's throne with confidence, to find grace to help in time of need. Jesus is there.[1]

Psalm 38

most of this psalm describes intense suffering. The psalmist is deeply wearied by coping with physical and mental pain. He feels guilty and regretful, reckoning his troubles began when he did something foolish and wrong, but he blames other people as well. Former friends are repelled by his condition (v 11). His enemies are closing in to ruin him (v 12).

There are no high points here, no moments when he rallies enough energy to praise God for his help in the past.[2] When he starts to pray he feels God is angry with him, inflicting the pain as discipline for sin (vs 1–3).

What is good is that this man is still talking to God. Somehow he hangs on to the hope that he still matters and God will pay attention to his catalogue of suffering (v 15). He confesses sin but is not yet at peace about it (v 18). He may be trying to decipher how much of the mess is his own fault and what stems from the hostility and lies of his enemies (vs 19,20).

Psalm 37 confronted us with the question: if we live in a right relationship with God, will we always flourish? Psalm 38 turns it round: if we are deep in pain and trouble, is it all God's punishment? The book of Job gives a very clear answer: no. Yet when people can see some failure that triggered an illness or disaster, they can find it hard to accept God's forgiveness because they find it hard to forgive themselves. Friends, with the strength to go on listening, can help convince a troubled person that God too is listening to their cry.

Praying for someone who is feeling as raw as this needs words chosen with great care. It is extremely easy to sound as if we too are blaming them.

1 Heb 4:15,16 **2 Ps 22:9,10**

... nor by power ...

'Lord, please give us that quietness of mind in which we can hear you speaking to us.'

2 Kings 6:24 - 7:2

Just occasionally in this history the 'royal tradition of certitude' is actually interrupted by an 'embarrassing footnote of hurt'.[1] The powerful are confronted by the consequences of their actions on the 'little people'.[2] What could be more embarrassing to the king than facing the agony of this woman? She had done the unthinkable and realised too late there had been a choice. Just as she is powerless to reverse what has been done, so also the king must admit his impotence (v 27).

The king is portrayed as a man who pays lip service to God's rule (v 30 and 5:7). But we've seen his unwillingness to deal with the profound malaise in Israel of corruption and anything-goes religion (3:1–3). With the typical response of the weak person he seeks a scapegoat for this frightful situation and identifies Elisha. No explanation is given. Perhaps he remembered Elisha's encouragement to be merciful to the Arameans who had not honoured their generous treatment (6:21). Elisha's response seems cowardly at first (v 32). Perhaps he senses the king's messenger may act first and think afterwards, and Elisha has an urgent message to transmit to the king describing an unimaginable reversal of circumstance in Samaria – no more horrors of starvation but cheap and plentiful food. Once more the prophet communicates the life-bringing 'word of the LORD' and lifts the curtain to new possibilities (7:1). Why does God not complete his judgement at this point? Why will the siege be lifted? Scripture bears constant witness to God's mercy and patience, especially on those 'little people' caught up in the actions of corrupt leaders.[3] Judgement on the king will come swiftly,[4] judgement on the cynical official (7:2) more swiftly still.

Pray today especially for those suffering terrible privations because of the wickedness of their leaders.

---

[1] Brueggemann [2] 1 Kings 21:17 [3] Jonah 4:2,10; 2 Pet 3:9 [4] 2 Kings 9:24–26

... but by my Spirit ...

'For God alone I wait silently; my deliverance comes from him.'[1]

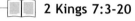

2 Kings 7:3-20

in no other Elisha episode is the 'alternative' narrative, history from the underside, told as vividly as here. We have everything that a good story needs: underdog heroes, subversive humour, tense dialogue, character development, and a resolution that comes full circle, bringing salvation for the people and terrible judgement on the official who shook his fist at God. We can almost hear the laughter as people visualise these four unheroic outcasts looming out of the dark in the enemy camp to the miraculous sounds of battle. The Hebrew puns with the words for 'lepers' and 'Egypt' (v 6), underlining the confusion that overcomes the Arameans, panic stricken as they imagine the Israelites have hired mercenary allies. The rout is complete (v 15).

Once again what is clear here is the tendency of those who hold power to obstruct and question the saving word of God (vs 2,12,13), while the despised people at the bottom of the heap are the means of salvation for others (v 9,15). As we've seen throughout this history, and as is clear in the wider 'big story' of Scripture, this is how God loves to work his reversals. He chooses to work through 'the despised things' to 'shame the strong'.[2] Of course, this is easy to state as proposition, but hard to live in practice. Eberhard Arnold of the Bruderhof movement has written, 'This is the root of grace: the dismantling of our power. Whenever even a little power rises up in us, the Spirit and the authority of God will retreat to the corresponding degree. In my estimation this is the single most important insight with regard to the kingdom of God'.[3]

'"We're not doing right. This is a day of good news and we are keeping it to ourselves."' Are we as outward looking with the gospel good news as the lepers were with theirs?

[1] Ps 62,REB [2] Luke 1:46–53 [3] Arnold, *Seeking Peace: Notes and Conversations*

sovereign in every detail

'Hidden in ... Scripture we find the kingdom of heaven ... unveiled to those who persevere in prayer with peaceful hearts.'[1]

2 Kings 8:1-29

Several commentators suggest that the conclusion of the story of the woman of Shunem (vs 1–6) belongs after 4:37 and after Elisha's death – notice that the unnamed king (possibly Jehu) asks Gehazi for memories of the prophet's deeds (v 4). The story seems to underline the truth that the influence of the person who listens faithfully to God can continue and bring blessing to others beyond his or her lifetime. This woman seems now to be a widow; seven years absence meant that her husband's lands reverted to the crown, and this time the king responds in a truly jubilee way to a vulnerable person's need.[2]

The second part of chapter 8 reverts to the royal history interrupted at chapter 3:3 by the 'alternative' history of God's doings through Elisha. The focus here is on the activity of God, through his prophet, in bringing about changes both in Damascus, the Aramean capital, and Samaria, capital of Israel. Among key facts that stand out among the 'royal' information of vs 16–24 are the succession of Jehoram in Judah, his marriage to Ahab's daughter Athaliah (v 18), his corrupt reign and loss of control over old enemies (v 22). His son Ahaziah, also deeply tainted with the evil of the Omri/Ahab dynasty, forms an alliance with Joram of Israel against the Arameans. As we shall see later, this is not only an alliance in life but also in death (9: 21–27). 'Then the man of God began to weep' (v 11). We have recognised many of the characteristics of the true prophet in Elisha. This moving passage reveals another, crucial, one. Those whom the Lord calls to speak his word of judgement will speak it with pain, anguish, grief.[3]

Do we share Elisha's anguish as we think of God's judgement on those who reject him or is it simply a cold doctrinal fact for us?

[1] **Nilus,** *Epistola 3295* [2] **Deut 15:1–4; see 1 Kings 21:7** [3] **Luke 13:34,35**

taking it further

key themes for study

Prophecy. These chapters are full of accounts of prophecies (1:6,16; 2:21; 3:15–19; 4:16,43; 7:1,2,18; 8:1,10,12,13). Usually an account is given of how what is predicted comes to pass.

The miraculous. Supernatural events occur: 21 incidents in all! They include revelation from the angel of the Lord (1:16); the calling down of fire from heaven (1:10,12), death in accord with a prophecy (1:17), the dividing of the Jordan (2:8,14), the birth of a son (4:17), the resurrection of the son (4:35), the feeding of 100 men (4:44), the healing of Naaman (5:14), Gehazi becoming leprous (5:27), and horses and chariots of fire around Elisha (6:17).

God's compassion for all. Jesus relates the ministry of Elijah and Elisha to the theme of God's concern for Gentiles (Luke 4:24–27); they are also seen as precursors of his own ministry.

for reflection/discussion

'Without history we have no knowledge of who we are or how we came to be; like victims of a collective amnesia, groping in the dark for our own identity' (Robert Daniels). Do you agree? How can we encourage interest in both biblical and church history?

'The Christian church in the West – mostly as complacent and market-driven as ancient Israel – may soon face catastrophe on the scale of the exile. These ancient history books ask us too, "How shall we then live?"' (Pauline Hoggarth.) What lessons can we learn from Kings? Can churches in the West learn from the values of Christians in other parts of the world?

for specific application

This section 'details starkly why the kingdom failed and the people were exiled despite God's covenant promises. It urgently engages people's imagination with what changes they must make if they are to look forward to a different future.' List what you expect to happen in your country over the next ten years. What would need to happen for things to be different?

songs of praise

a s Christmas approaches we turn to Luke's Gospel to be reminded of the fundamental truth at the heart of our faith – that God became flesh among us. The story – and its celebration – is so familiar to us. But the Scriptures invite us to see things through new eyes. This is actually what Luke was offering to Theophilus (1:3; he was probably a wealthy Gentile who was sponsoring the production of the Gospel). Theophilus had heard much about Jesus, and Luke wanted to communicate 'the *certainty* of the things you have been taught' (1:4) – to help him see below the surface, grasp the inner meaning, and know the 'security' of the message about Jesus. Pray for that 'new look' for yourself this Christmas. Luke has surprises in store.

In the ancient world people believed that the events surrounding the birth of a famous figure contained signs of what the child was to become. That is why Luke tells the story so fully, and underlines the supernatural happenings that marked Jesus' birth. We hear three separate angelic messages here, not to mention a roaring praise-song from the whole heavenly army (2:14). But, beyond the angels, where are the great men? Where are the kings and philosophers, by whom greatness is usually measured and recognised? They appear, for sure, but in this story they are cast right outside their usual role. Instead think about the role played here by teenagers (two), by pensioners (four), by social rejects (a whole group, near Bethlehem), and by the Holy Spirit, who makes a sudden and dramatic re-entry into Israel's history in connection with the births of these two babies. It's not just the mothers who keep such 'poor' company, but also the Holy Spirit of God himself, who bursts into prophetic song on the lips of the poor, and invites us to sing along.

further reading
I would recommend Dinah Roe Kendall's wonderful pictures of these chapters in her book *Allegories of Heaven*, Piquant, 2002.

Steve Motyer

the God of surprises

Imagine God saying to you: are you ready for me to turn your life upsidedown? React to that question, in prayer.

Luke 1:1-17

i t was already a special day for Zechariah the priest. Not only was his order on duty in Jerusalem – something which only happened twice a year – but he himself had been chosen to offer the incense at the morning sacrifice, a once-in-a-lifetime privilege. This meant entering the Holy Place itself, alone, and spreading the incense on the glowing red coals on the altar right in front of the veil before the Holy of Holies.

It was a moment of great solemnity, and of fear. Only on the Day of Atonement, once a year, did anyone penetrate further into the presence of God, when the High Priest went behind the veil. No wonder this poor rustic priest was terrified when an angel suddenly appeared next to the altar of incense.

And the message? God had something completely different in mind for Zechariah than just the awesome privilege of serving him in this way. Zechariah, it seems, had long since come to terms with his childlessness, and his wife Elizabeth was probably miles from his thoughts as he spread the incense. But God had not forgotten all their agonised prayers uttered through the long years of their youth and middle age, and was about to step in, dramatically. They are to have a son, a mighty prophet, consecrated to God like a Nazirite (1:15),[1] who will prepare Israel to receive her Lord.

Why could they not have had the baby years before, and been spared all that pain? Because our God is a God of surprises, who acts in *his* way and at *his* time, and asks us to follow. Are we ready?

Review the ruts in your life. Are you stuck in any? Could God be calling you to adventurous faith, a new beginning with him? Be ready to be surprised.

[1] **Compare Num 6:1–8**

hearing God the wrong way

As years advance, we become 'set in our ways'. This can be an obstacle to our continued responsiveness to God …

Luke 1:18-25

Zechariah's response to the angel's message is very sobering. Mary asks a similar question later (v 34), but the spirit in which she asks it is completely different. The promise to Zechariah and Elizabeth was related directly to their lifelong childlessness (vs 7,13), and Zechariah simply refuses to believe it. 'How can I be sure of this?' should probably be translated, 'How could I ever experience that?' (v 18). He has long since 'come to terms' with his childlessness, and become comfortable with his life – and so can't accept this disturbance to his elderly peace, even though announced by Gabriel, the 'Strength of God'. So, if he can't say anything better than that, it would be better for him not to speak at all!

Elizabeth stays quiet, too – but for a very different reason. Why did she go into hiding as soon as she became pregnant (v 24)? Why did she not shout verse 25 in the marketplace? We can only speculate. But clearly the pain of her childlessness is still living with her. It is her 'disgrace among the people'. She has not suppressed the pain, like Zechariah. To proclaim her extraordinary pregnancy would end her disgrace, but it would bring agony to all the other childless women to whom she has been a mother in their grief, and for whom there will be no such deliverance. She will not open her mouth, until the Holy Spirit does when Mary arrives (vs 41–45).

And Zechariah will speak again too: God will restore speech to him when he is ready to speak words of grace and praise, responding positively to the wonderful thing that God is doing in his family.

Pray for grace in older life: not to be a Zechariah, closed to the unexpected that God may delight to give to his church, but to be an Elizabeth, sensitive to others' needs.

hearing God

When have you known that 'God is with you' in your life?
Perhaps make a few jottings, identifying times and occasions.

Luke 1:26-38

Luke's Gospel is remarkable for the way in which it begins with two babies, not just with one. The first will be a prophet, filled with the Holy Spirit from before birth, turning Israel back to God and preparing them for the Lord. The second will be the new son of David, the Son of the Most High, ruling over the house of Jacob for ever (vs 32,33).

At the end of the chapter, Zechariah will compare and contrast the two babies, and explain their significance. Here, however, Mary could be forgiven if she didn't grasp the full meaning of Gabriel's message. After all, she's just a peasant girl, probably only a young teenager. 'Humble' is her own word to describe herself (v 48). Luke does this repeatedly in his Gospel – shows how God, in Jesus, is interested in the people others bypass, the nobodies at the bottom of the pile who have no power or voice. Mary is one such.

And here she is, greeted by Gabriel with these wonderful words, 'Greetings, favoured one! The Lord is with you!' (NRSV). It had never occurred to Mary to think of herself as 'favoured' by God – that's for the great, who don't live in obscure villages like Nazareth but rule from mighty palaces. And in what sense is the Lord 'with' her? That's usually a privilege for prophets and kings… Gabriel explains. Her favoured status will lead her into rejection and disgrace, into pregnancy before marriage excused by a story few will believe, a virgin pregnancy caused by the Holy Spirit – because she will be mother to the King!

Mary accepts it. 'I'm the Lord's slave-girl', she says. 'I'm ready for what you say' (v 38, my translation).

Are you ready to be 'with' the Lord in disgrace, hardship, rejection – adopted into the humble family of Jesus of Nazareth?

look away from me, Lord

What do you really want to talk to God about today? What is the issue most on your heart?

Psalm 39

as in Psalm 38, the psalmist is suffering greatly and believes that God is rebuking and disciplining him for sin (vs 8–11). This psalmist however is at a different stage in the human experience of suffering. He feels angry and wants to confront God. How can he do it?

He tried bottling it up in case he gave ammunition to God's critics, but he felt like a furnace about to explode (vs 2,3). So now he pours it out in prayer.

He begins at a safe distance, questioning the meaning of life. The Hebrew word translated 'a breath' (vs 5,11) and 'in vain' (v 6) is the key word 'vanity' or 'meaningless' in Ecclesiastes. Like that preacher, this psalmist focuses on the brevity and fragility of human life on earth and he asks God what he is supposed to make of it.[1] By the middle of the psalm his personal suffering becomes more dominant. Like Job, he feels that an all-powerful God holds all the trump cards and that he is being punished more harshly than he can bear. Like a bullied child he pleads for mercy but longs for his tormentor to look away and not notice him any more.[2]

To the believer who is fit and well and enjoying a relatively untroubled life, passages like this psalm can be puzzling and embarrassing. There is a tendency to explain them away or hurry to a New Testament text about resurrection and joy. But many people going through dark and painful times find them a lifeline. They give permission for us to turn painful anger into prayer and imply that God will be there at the other end, listening but offering no pat answers.

It is good to meditate on the cross during good times in life, and store away a sense of God's compassionate love which we can draw on when painful days arrive.

[1] Ps 90:12; Eccl 2:12–16 [2] Job 30:20–22; 10:18–22

the voice of prophecy

Should religion and politics be kept separate? Reflect on your views on this, and your reasons for them.

Luke 1:39-56

One of Luke's special interests in both his books (this Gospel and Acts), is *prophecy.* For several hundred years there had been no prophets in Israel. But with the coming of Christ, the Holy Spirit returned, prophecy was reborn, and eventually the whole church was filled with the Spirit of prophecy at Pentecost.

Here it all begins! And for Luke there was special pleasure in recording that the first to be filled with the Spirit, and speak from God, was a *woman*, Elizabeth of Judah. She shouts a 'loud cry' (NRSV) of greeting to Mary (v 42), discerning her pregnancy without being told, realising its significance ('the mother of my Lord!'), praising Mary for her faith, and incidentally announcing her own pregnancy at the same time. There must have been a huge stir in the village – at least among the women. Doubtless the men dismissed it all as women's nonsense!

Then Mary timidly speaks. Had she been composing this song of praise on her long walk from Nazareth? She sees so clearly what it means; that God has chosen people like her (and Elizabeth) through whom to 'perform mighty deeds with his arm' (v 51): it means a reversal of the usual power structures, a putting-down of the great, a lifting-up of the poor, the rejection of the self-sufficient and provision for the helpless. This is political dynamite! The kingdom of God, coming with Mary's baby, subverts all earthly kingdoms, renders all rulers accountable, and introduces a whole new order of loyalty, because *God* has stepped in to 'help his servant Israel' where earthly kings cannot save (v 54).

In what ways might loyalty to Mary's baby lead us to challenge earthly political powers? Pray about this in the light of your circumstances.

the time has come

We all look back on significant moments, points in time crucial in the story of our lives. What are they for you?

Luke 1:57-66

Zechariah made a mess of it last time. He came face to face with the angel Gabriel and blew it. The most vital moment in his life, and he failed his God. But during the long months of Elizabeth's pregnancy, his thoughts moved from self-recrimination to thankfulness for the coming baby. And when Mary arrived with her news – what a whole new perspective opened up! And then the birth, and the circumcision, when their baby would be formally named. It seems as though Zechariah was a quiet man, anyway, because he had not communicated Gabriel's instruction about the name (v 13) to any but Elizabeth. But this time he took a mischievous delight in breaking convention, and warmly embracing God's new thing: 'His name is John!' (v 63).

And then – hard on the heels of his obedience to Gabriel's message – his speech returns. What will he say? Luke keeps us in suspense, and records first the *effect* of Zechariah's words : 'Awe came upon all their neighbours, and all these words were passed on throughout the hill country of Judea. Everyone who heard them kept the words in mind saying, "What then will this child be? The hand of the Lord is with him!"' (my translation). Verses 65,66 should probably be translated this way, emphasising people's reaction to Zechariah's first utterance. For once again it was a *prophetic* message, inspired by the Holy Spirit (v 67). This time, led by the Spirit, Zechariah did not mess up. His words gripped, and compelled attention, and introduced his son's special prophetic ministry, preparing the way for the one who would follow. The essence is in verse 64: 'he spoke, praising God'. So simple, but so difficult.

Pray that the Spirit of God will lead you, when your next decisive moment comes. And pray that this Christmas may be marked by real, simple praise.

Zechariah speaks

Many biblical verses are alluded to in Zechariah's song.1 Ask God to fill your heart with his truth.

Luke 1:67-80

uke uses Zechariah's marvellous two-part song to bring the first part of the story to a powerful conclusion and to prepare for the next. The second part (vs 76–79) explains the relationship between the two baby boys – the one just born, the other just about to be. Here, for the first time, the great term 'Lord' (*kyrios*) is applied to *Jesus:* 'you will go before the Lord to prepare the way for him' (v 76). In the coming of Jesus, *the Lord* is coming to Israel, bringing salvation and forgiveness, and the fulfilment of all the covenant promises.

And that's the theme of the first part (vs 68–75): the covenant promises given by God through Abraham and the prophets, that he would bring sure salvation to his people, rescuing them from their enemies and enabling them to live rightly before him. In verse 72 Zechariah plays subtly on his own and John's names: the Lord promised to 'show mercy' (John means 'Yahweh is merciful') and to 'remember his covenant' (Zechariah means 'Yahweh remembers'). He doesn't hesitate to say it: all the promises are now being fulfilled, the great 'horn of salvation' is rising from the house of David, and deliverance is at hand.2

For Zechariah, it was all focused on Israel. This is a very *Old Testament* prophecy, full of language and allusions to passages from the Hebrew Scriptures. But if Zechariah couldn't see beyond Israel, Luke could. He knew that God's plans are world-embracing. In the very last verse a hint is dropped: 'to shine on those living in darkness …' This allusion to Isaiah 9:1 reminds us of the *Gentiles* on whom the light will shine also. And so the stage is set.

Use this passage again, but specifically now as your own Christmas prayer, rather than as an object of study. Apply verse 76 as a prayer to yourself.

1 Ps 18:17; 111:9; 132:17; Isa 9:2; Mic 7:20 2 Ps 132:17

fulfilment

Reflect on the politics of the Christmas story. As you read, ask yourself what it says about worldly political power.

Luke 2:1-20

Once again we meet Luke's wonderful contrast between the great and the nobodies. The mighty emperor Augustus thought it was time for a tax census. But God thought the time had come for one insignificant couple, in a far-flung corner of Augustus' empire, to travel south so that David's heir could be born in David's city. And while the crowds jostled around Bethlehem, cursing the distant emperor for causing such chaos, a teenage girl, crammed into the animal quarters of her husband's family home, gave birth to a baby boy, and lovingly laid him in a manger.

But behind the veil of time heaven was in riot. Out on the hills – where they lived because they were regarded as 'unclean' by religious folk – some shepherds were suddenly confronted by a great light, and an angel talking of a baby, and a heavenly army singing about peace. 'Host' in verse 13 should certainly be translated 'army': this is the angelic army which occasionally goes into battle,[1] and which Jesus refused to call to his aid in Gethsemane.[2] If God were to take a leaf out of Augustus' book, he would send this army to *compel* obedience, to *demand* his dues, to *destroy* his enemies. But he does not 'save' that way. He does not believe in redemptive violence, the politics of the quick 'strike' to set things right. He sends a baby, tells his army to *sing* – and communicates the good news to the lowliest on earth, to those who will certainly be ignored when they tell what they have seen.

But only where this baby is embraced will there be peace: only there is war stilled, and sin forgiven, and love secure.

Respond in imagination: break the social barrier, and join the shepherds. Then go with them to find the baby, telling them what the angels' message means. What's their response?

1 Eg 2 Sam 5:24 2 Matt 26:53

suddenly in his temple ...

Think about the Temple in Jerusalem. Imagine yourself there.
See the people, hear the shofar, smell the sacrifices...

 Luke 2:21-40

two episodes now follow, both set in the Temple. Zechariah gave the hint when he alluded to Malachi 3:1 in 1:76 – the Lord suddenly comes to his Temple, in fulfilment of that prophecy.

But whereas people expected a *glorious, powerful* coming, the reality is very different. It needs special, prophetic discernment to set apart this young couple, with their baby, from all the others entering the Temple that day.

Why did they come? Luke subtly combines allusions to three Old Testament themes: the ritual of purification (2:22a), the redemption of the firstborn (2:23), and the presentation to the Lord (2:22b). *Like every other Jewish baby,* Jesus has made his mother 'unclean' by the process of childbirth, and she needs to be purified.[1] And *like every other Jewish firstborn male,* Jesus must be 'redeemed' because he is 'holy to the LORD'.[2] But we already know of the unique sense in which he is 'holy to the LORD':[3] and so, *unlike every other Jewish baby,* Mary and Joseph take their firstborn to the Temple to 'present him to the Lord', re-enacting Hannah's presentation of Samuel to the sanctuary at Shiloh.[4] They give him back *to* the Lord, because he is a unique gift *from* the Lord, and from now on he 'belongs' in the Temple (and thus we are prepared for the next 'Temple' story in Luke 2).

But Simeon sees the sword coming. To save the Gentiles as well as Israel (2:32) the Temple – that bastion of Jewish exclusiveness – will have to go. Luke will go on to tell this sad story.

Now think and feel your way into Mary's heart. What does she feel as she hears Simeon's words? Do you fear what the future may bring? Bring your feelings to the Lord.

[1] **Lev 12:1–8** [2] **Exod 13:2; Num 18:15,16** [3] **Luke 1:35** [4] **1 Sam 1:28**

.ole in a year: ZECHARIAH 7,8 REVELATION 19

'about my Father's business'

Review the year past before God, and begin to formulate some prayer resolutions for the year ahead.

Luke 2:41-52

have you ever felt slightly embarrassed by Jesus' apparent thoughtlessness towards his parents – not letting them know that he wanted to stay on in the Temple? Don't feel embarrassed. As Luke tells it, the action in 2:22 prepares for this incident. Jesus' parents seem to have forgotten that they actually 'presented' him in the Temple, so that he belongs there in a unique way. Perhaps inevitably, they have developed a certain possessiveness towards him. 'Your father and I…', says Mary. 'Didn't you know that I had to be about my Father's business?', replies Jesus (author's translation). Of course they *did* know this – they had themselves performed the action which expressed Jesus' unique 'holiness' before his *heavenly* Father. They of all people knew that, uniquely, he was 'the Son of God'!

We can so easily domesticate the sacred, lay hold of it, claim it for 'ours', whether it be 'our' family, or house, or church, or job, or future. Even though in the past we may have joyfully surrendered all these to the Lord, possessiveness can creep back in. We can start to clutch things to us, in a way which stops *us* from 'being about the Father's business'.

For we, too, are 'holy to the Lord': not of course in Jesus' special way, serving the Lord out of that unique Father-Son relationship, but *called by him* to 'be about his business' with the same single-minded zeal that kept Jesus glued to the Temple while his parents wandered off. As a new year approaches, let's renew our commitment to be 'holy to the Lord', belonging wholly to him, body, heart and mind, within the *temple* of all our relationships and tasks.

Give yourself afresh to the Lord today, renewing your commitment to belong to him, to think, speak and act for him, in all that lies ahead of you in 2004.

taking it further

key themes for study

Signs of Jesus' significance. 'In the ancient world people believed that the events surrounding the birth of a famous figure contained signs of what the child was to become.' What do you think is conveyed about Jesus in the events Luke portrays?

Knowing with certainty. Commenting on 1:4, Steve Motyer suggests that Luke wants to help Theophilus 'see below the surface, grasp the inner meaning, and know the "security" of the message about Jesus'. Luke's basis for this in thorough individual research and eyewitnesses' testimonies (1:1,3) encourages confidence in his gospel's reliability. But beyond this, Luke calls us to ponder the significance of these facts (2:19).

Fulfilment of prophecy. In his portrayal of events, Luke has clearly been greatly influenced by the prophecies of Isaiah, especially his poetic depiction of the arrival of good news (Isa 40:9; 52:7), of captives set free, and the coming of great joy (Isa 51:11) and salvation (Isa 52:7,10), due to the arrival of the reign of God.

Power and the powerless. Steve Motyer stresses the role played in the narrative by the marginalised. The Son of God has come 'to preach good news to the poor' (4:18), to those without status or worldly power. Note also the contrast between 'Caesar Augustus' (2:1) and 'Christ the Lord' (2:11): one rules and creates the 'pax romana' by force and threat of war, the other brings 'good news of great joy' and peace – lasting peace.

for reflection/discussion

One has 'come to us from heaven to shine on those living in darkness and in the shadow of death, and to guide our feet into the path of peace' (1:78, 79). How do we repsond to this?

for specific application

'Our God is a God of surprises, who acts in *his* way and at *his* time'. Bring to God disappointments from the past, and affirm your openness to receiving gifts he may yet have in store for you.

responding to the Rescuer

Relax as you read this psalm. There is good news today.

Psalm 40

a life-changing conversion, recovery from grief or healing at death's door? Many experiences in the spiritual life could fit this powerful description of being lifted out of a muddy pit and set down on firm open ground (v 2). Much of this psalm is a response to God for such a moment.

Commentators think it came to be associated with Israel's kings, thanking God for salvation on behalf of the whole nation. David was chosen to replace King Saul because Saul sacrificed to God while directly disobeying him.[1] Sacrifices were intended to be signs of dying to sinfulness and giving oneself to God. God is interested in the real thing, not just the sign.[2] So the king declares his ears are open (v 6) and he is attending to what the Law says, including its requirements for kings (v 7).[3]

The New Testament sees Christ as the King who supremely came to do God's will. His death was the one real sacrifice for sin to which all the earlier signs pointed. We, who are represented by him, are promised that the Holy Spirit will write God's law on our hearts.[4] Verses 6–8 can be our own response to God, warning us not to confuse religious show with an obedient heart.

The psalm does not end on the heights. As in most computer games, while we are rejoicing in one victory, another battle appears on screen. Having waited intensely for God (v 1) and praised generously when help came (v 9), individuals and churches become stronger and bolder to press God not to withhold mercy (v 11) and not to delay (v 17) when the next need arises.

The psalm assumes kings go into battle. There is no lack of new songs sung in church today, but leaders need able to connect them with fresh stories of a God who saves.

1 **1 Sam 15:22** 2 **Ps 51:16; Hos 6:6** 3 **Deut 17:18–20** 4 **Heb 10:8–10**

Keith Civval

living with a biblical
model of family

how important is the biblical model of family in our modern world? Is it something that we, as Christians, should strive to uphold as a key building block in the structure of society or should we accept its diminishing importance? The absence of any specific ordinance in Scripture to establish and maintain nuclear family life should not disguise the fact that in the Old and New Testaments family is not just viewed as culturally normative but as a divine provision for the well-being of all people. In the beginning God said: 'It is not good for the man to be alone. I will make a helper suitable for him'.[1] From Adam and Eve, to Noah (who was told by God to take his whole family into the ark), and Abram and Sarai, right through to Mary and Joseph, children were brought into the world and reared in a stable family with two parents. The Psalms and Proverbs also testify that family life is part of God's blessing and provision.[2]

> *"Jesus ... was born into and grew up in an earthly family, living in obedience to his parents"*

Jesus, despite the depth of relationship with his heavenly Father, was born into and grew up in an earthly family, living in obedience to his parents.[3] On the cross he made special provision for his mother who was deprived of her son through death.[4] Paul, even though he was a single man, was particularly keen to stress the importance of family life. A church leader, he said, must be 'the husband of but one wife' and 'manage his own family well and see that his children obey him with proper respect'.[5] And, in writing to the Ephesians and Colossians he stresses sound family relationships as a foundational principle of Christian living.[6] As with many other aspects of the Judaeo-Christian tradition, family life has long been part of our own culture, even if it is not seen explicitly as part of God's divine provision. Today, however, this tradition is under very real threat. According to the latest government statistics over 40 per cent of children are now born to (and over half are conceived by) unmarried parents.[7] A quarter of all children in the UK live in families with a lone parent – twice as many as 20 years earlier.[8] Why does the reporting of this sort of statistic not create a national outcry? Just imagine the reaction to news that 40 per cent of apples consumed in this country were stolen from supermarket shelves! Perhaps this is because there is no perceived crime against the person – no apparent loser. But what about the children? According to recent research by Civitas[9] children living without their natural fathers are more likely to live in poverty and deprivation; are more likely to have emotional or mental problems; have more trouble in school; tend to have more trouble getting along with others; have higher risk of health problems; are at greater risk of suffering physical, emotional or sexual abuse; and are more likely to run away from home. Corresponding problems arise for teenagers and young adults living without their natural fathers. This (secular) piece of research concludes, 'The weight of evidence indicates that the traditional family based upon a married father and mother is still the best environment for raising children, and it forms the soundest basis for the wider society'. Scripture Union is developing new ways of supporting family life; mindful of the fact that we need to balance the ideal biblical model with the pastoral reality we find in our churches today: broken marriages, single-parent families and more. There is no easy answer to this challenge but with God's grace we should seek to build his kingdom on earth on the foundations of his Word.

Keith Civval

1 **Gen 2:18** 2 **Ps 68:6; 127:3–5; Prov 11:29; 15:27** 3 **Luke 2:39–51**
4 **John 19:26,27** 5 **1 Tim 3:2–4** 6 **Eph 6:1–4; Col 3:20,21** 7 **Review of the Registrar General on births and patterns of family building in England and Wales, 2001** 8 *Living in Britain,* **2001** 9 *Experiments in Living: The Fatherless Family*

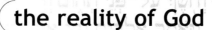

the reality of God

We have almost no information about Habakkuk or his life. The Babylonians are in the ascendant and this places the book in the period soon after the battle of Carchemish in 605BC and a few years before the fall of Jerusalem in 586BC. The reigns of Manasseh and Amon had seen a turning from God and the breakdown of social order. The reforms of Josiah had been superficial and short-lived. Violence, oppression and injustice were rife.

As Habakkuk struggles with this he gives us a unique insight into the prophetic mind. Here we see the agonised questioning and prayer that lies behind the prophetic message. It is forged in reflection on the state of society and the events of the day rather than in a spiritual vacuum or isolated piety. The prophet is one who engages with the world and who seeks God's mind on what he sees. This is not a cold, analytical process; Habakkuk displays strong emotion and deep concern. It is in the depth of his pain and doubt that he encounters God and hears his word. Would-be prophets should perhaps take note! It is no easy matter to bring the word of the Lord. When Habakkuk describes his message as a burden (1:1, AV), he reflects reality.

The world of Habakkuk is not unlike our own. We, too, live with violence. In many nations we see a growing underclass of the poor and the powerless. Children, women and the old are exploited and abused. Asylum seekers and refugees are seen as a threat. Unborn children are aborted without too much thought about the moral consequences. Racial tension and violence towards minorities is ever present. There are wars, muggings, domestic violence. If we are sensitive like Habakkuk, we will protest. Where is God in this? Why does he not act to protect the innocent and establish justice? Why does a holy God apparently turn a blind eye to evil?

Habakkuk reminds us that questioning God is acceptable. Indeed, arguing the case with God is the best way to deal with the fears, doubts and uncertainties that life so often raises. The answer we receive may, however, not be the one that we expect. Habakkuk got rather more than he bargained for. But in the process he learned that God is working out his purposes even in unlikely and, to human eyes, unacceptable ways. However hard it may be to believe it, we can be sure that he is in control. Habakkuk's journey from fear and doubt to a faith that will hold on to God even in the desperate times is not an easy one. But for the many in our world who find faith hard it is a potent source of encouragement.

This is ultimately a book not about human doubts and questions but about the way in which God moves forward his purposes in the world. At a point when the promises of God to Abraham must have seemed in doubt, the people are pointed back to the God of Abraham, Isaac and Jacob, to the God of the exodus and Sinai. This book encourages us to see the world through different eyes, to re-evaluate our simplistic analyses and to stand in awe of a God who is bigger than we imagined. It gives us the hope to believe, even in the darkest days, that God will establish his reign of justice and that the day will come when the earth shall be filled with the knowledge of the glory of God (2:14).

further reading
If you want to dig deeper into Habakkuk, David Prior (*The Message of Joel, Micah and Habakkuk*, Bible Speaks Today, IVP) is a solid guide. Martyn Lloyd-Jones (*From Fear to Faith*, IVP) relates it to the personal journey and Elizabeth Achtemeier (*Nahum-Malachi*, Interpretation, John Knox) never fails to stimulate with fresh insights.

John Grayston

danger - God at work

Hold the world before God, reflecting on society as you see it. Ask him to give you a new perspective.

Habakkuk 1:1-17

habakkuk's problem is an age-old one. It is the problem of Job and of Psalm 73. Why does evil prosper in a world which is under the control of a holy and just God? In Habakkuk's world of violence and oppression the law is powerless to protect the innocent or hold the guilty accountable. We may identify with his questioning. As we noted in the introduction, there are many parallels with our own world, and if we are remotely sensitive they trouble us.

In the face of the problem we can resort to instant judgements – normally those which find a scapegoat whom we can demonise, thus conveniently letting us off the hook. The response which Habakkuk receives from God illustrates, however, the complexity of the problem. Habakkuk has not seen anything yet! Worse is to come. The Babylonians, renowned for their brutality, are on the way. Habakkuk, having taken the problem to God – perhaps a more mature response than many of us would have made – is left with an even greater question. At one level the Babylonians are God's answer and Habakkuk can rejoice in that. But does this not leave God condoning a still greater evil? How can a God of infinite purity tolerate this (v 13)? Is he not being untrue to his own character? The question is left hanging in the air, the resolution left to another day. How like our own experience of God! This chapter asks us to rethink our view of the world. Who might the modern equivalent of the ruthless, godless, violent Babylonians be? What if Al-Qaeda, for example, were God's wake-up call to the West? Too simplistic? Perhaps. But dare we even raise the question?

Take some time to look at the world again. Where might God be at work in unexpected ways?

silence - God is here

'I wait for the LORD, my soul waits, and in his word I put my hope.'[1]

Habakkuk 2:1-20

more light emerges. Things are moving forward to a designated end (vs 2,3). Contrary to all the impressions, God is working his purposes out, even through the most unlikely of instruments. No doubt he still is, if only we have the faith and vision to see beyond the immediate circumstances and our own limited perceptions. Sometimes there is little more we can do than to hold on to the conviction that God is working and wait. Waiting is a key theme in Scripture – a hard lesson for us who live in an age of instant gratification.[2]

The Babylonians may be God's instrument to move forward his larger purposes and to call his covenant people back to himself. But that does not give them carte blanche to behave as they will (vs 9,12). They too will be held accountable; for their pride and arrogance (vs 4,5), for their violence and aggression (vs 6–13), for the way they have ravaged creation (v 17). (This may give us cause for thought given the nature of modern warfare with its increased impact on the natural environment.) The folly of trusting in false gods will be exposed (vs 18–20); they cannot provide spiritual sustenance or moral values. Whoever we are and whatever our role in the plans of God there is a requirement to worship him alone and live by his values. This is a challenge to the covenant community as much as to the foreign oppressor. Where are the modern idols that control our value systems (vs 18,19) and lead us away from the life of faith which alone can save us (v 4)? If our ultimate motivation is corporate profit or private gain, personal aggrandisement or national conquest, we have succumbed to the worship of another god.

Hear the call to come and be silent before God (v 20).[3] Respond in your own way.

1 Ps 130:5 2 Ps 25:5; 27:14; 40:1; Isa 40:31; Lam 3:24–26 3 Ps 46:10

hang on - God is coming

Come to the Bible today with a sense of expectancy. Prepare for a fresh vision of God.

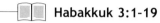

Habakkuk 3:1-19

as we are silent before God the unthinkable happens – he comes in glory. Exactly what experience Habakkuk had which prompted this song of praise is unclear. What *is* clear is that as he continues wrestling with God he reaches a point where he sees things differently.

Initially he sees God in his glory (vs 2–15) – the vision and the language used similar to that which describes some of the most significant events in the relationship of God with Israel.[1] Here is raw power and splendour; this is no cosy, manageable God. There is perhaps in today's church too little understanding of this aspect of God's character. How do we respond to this picture of God? How do we capture a sense of awe before a holy and powerful God while also holding on to the idea of a loving Father?

Habakkuk is physically weighed down, weakened by the crushing sense of God's presence which is too much too bear. Awe-inspiring this may be, but it is not destructive. It actually brings him to the point of supreme faith. This God knows what he is doing and he can do it. In the face of such a revelation, questions may remain but trust takes over. And what trust! All that makes life liveable is removed; the staples of life are gone, and yet Habakkuk holds on to God and, amid the deprivation, rejoices (v 18). Not many of us will have experienced such loss. In what ways can those of us who enjoy more comfortable existences hold on to such a God? How can we support those – in our own communities and in other parts of the world – who have literally lost everything except their faith in God? How can we learn from them?

Pray that your own Christian community might have a vision of God that is this big and this life-changing.

[1] **Eg Deut 33; Judg 5:1–12; Exod 19:16–20**

taking it further

key themes for study
God's apparent injustice. Habakkuk raises the question, 'Why does a holy God apparently turn a blind eye to evil?' And how can he use a 'ruthless, godless, violent' nation to judge his people? The answer that 'they too will be held accountable' is probably not the one the prophet wanted to hear!

Idolatry. John Grayston remarks that 'if our ultimate motivation is corporate profit or private gain, personal aggrandisement or national conquest, we have succumbed to the worship of another god.' The New Testament as well as the Old has much to teach about idolatry (see 1 Cor 10:14–22; Col 3:5; 1 John 5:21; Rev 22:15).

Waiting. Habakkuk stations himself on the ramparts, waiting to hear what God will say to him (2:1). The answer calls for faith (2:4), which involves faithful perseverance. His vision described in chapter 3 emphasises that God is awesome, and knows what he is doing. In the midst of terrible destruction, and although not all his questions are answered, Habakkuk is able to affirm his trust and even rejoice in the greatness of his God (3:17–19).

for reflection/discussion
'For the earth will be filled with the knowledge of the glory of the LORD, as the waters cover the sea' (2:14).

In Habakkuk 'we see the agonised questioning and prayer that lies behind the prophetic message.' What implications does this have for you?

for specific application
'It is in the depth of his pain and doubt that [Habakkuk] encounters God and hears his word.' Do not run away from the nagging doubts and emotional wounds you feel in your heart. Bring them to God your Father in the confidence that he is big enough to handle them – and to bring you healing.

subscription order form

You may order your notes
- from your local Christian bookshop
- from your church Bible reading representative
- by post from Scripture Union Mail Order* at the address below
- order online at www.scriptureunion.org.uk

Scripture Union Mail Order, PO Box 5148, Milton Keynes MLO, MK2 2YX
Mail order: 01908 856006 Enquiries: 01908 856000 Fax: 01908 856020

Quarterly Bible reading notes *Prices increase by £1 from 1 January 2004*	Quantity	UK	Europe	Rest of the world
Encounter with God		£10.00	£13.00	£15.00

Please begin my annual subscription in ☐ Jan ☐ Apr ☐ Jul ☐ Oct

Payment with order is required

Total: £ ....

Gift to Scripture Union's evangelistic work: £ ....

Total amount enclosed: £ ....

Name ....

Address..

....Postcode..

Tel No .... Email ....

I enclose my postal order/cheque** made payable to Scripture Union

Please debit my Mastercard/Switch/Visa** Card Number:

Expiry Date: ☐☐☐☐   Valid from / Switch Issue No: ☐☐☐

Date ☐☐☐☐☐☐   Cardholder Name ....

Signature..

allow 28 days for delivery 　　*** delete as applicable*　　　　EWG034

Scripture Union publishes a full range of Bible reading materials for people of all ages.
For a brochure, please telephone 01908 856006; visit www.scriptureunion.org.uk
or write to SU Mail Order, PO Box 5148, Milton Keynes MLO, MK2 2YX

We would like to keep in touch with you by placing you on our mailing list.
If you would prefer not, please tick here: ☐
Scripture Union does not sell or lease its mailing list.

To the retailer: This coupon will be redeemed by Scripture Union provided it has
been used for this offer and returned fully completed to STL Customer Services Dept,
PO Box 300, Kingstown Broadway, Carlisle, Cumbria CA3 0QS.